CONTENTS

ACKNOWLEDGEMENTS

MAP OF SCOTLAND

THE ROYAL SUCCESSION

INTRODUCTION: FAMILIES AT WAR

PART ONE – THE SCOTTISH SUCCESSION CRISIS

1. KINGS AND NOBLES BEFORE 1286
2. THE INTERREGNUM AND GREAT
   CAUSE, 1286–92
3. KING JOHN I OF SCOTLAND, 1292–96
4. THE SCOTTISH REBELLION, 1296-1302
5. SECRECY AND MURDER, 1302–06

PART TWO – THE BRUCE CAUSE

1. THE BRUCES' SCOTTISH WAR, 1306–10
2. THE TRIUMPHANT ROAD TO
   BANNOCKBURN, 1310–14
3. IRELAND, THE SUCCESSION AND TREASON,
   1315–20
4. IN SEARCH OF CLOSURE, 1320-27
5. UNFINISHED BUSINESS, 1327–29

PART THREE – A WAR WON IN DEFEAT

1. THE RETURN OF BALLIOL, 1329–32
2. HALIDON HILL TO CHÂTEAU
      GAILLARD, 1332–34
3. MURRAY'S WAR FOR SCOTLAND, 1335–38
4. ROBERT STEWARD'S LIEUTENANCY, 1338–41
5. THE UNCERTAIN ROAD TO NEVILLE'S
      CROSS, 1341–46
6. TIME RUNS OUT FOR BALLIOL, 1347–56

CONCLUSION: WINNING THE PEACE
– AFTER 1357

A GUIDE TO FURTHER READING

LIST OF ILLUSTRATIONS, MAPS AND DIAGRAMS

INDEX

THE SCOTTISH
CIVIL WAR

The Bruces & the Balliols
& the War for Control of Scotland, 1286–1356

Michael Penman

January 2003 .

THE SCOTTISH CIVIL WAR

*The Bruces & the Balliols
& the War for Control of
Scotland, 1286–1356*

MICHAEL PENMAN

TEMPUS

First published 2002

PUBLISHED IN THE UNITED KINGDOM BY:
Tempus Publishing Ltd
The Mill, Brimscombe Port
Stroud, Gloucestershire GL5 2QG

PUBLISHED IN THE UNITED STATES OF AMERICA BY:
Tempus Publishing Inc.
2 Cumberland Street
Charleston, SC 29401

British Library Cataloguing in Publication Data.
A catalogue record for this book is available from the British Library.

ISBN 0 7524 2319 3

Typesetting and origination by Tempus Publishing
Printed in Great Britain by Midway Colour Print, Wiltshire

ACKNOWLEDGEMENTS

As this short book is based in part upon the content of a course I teach at the University of Stirling, I would first like to thank the many students who have already taken *Scotland in the Age of Wallace and Bruce* and brought a number of new approaches and ideas to the subject. I am very grateful, too, to Dr Fiona Watson of Stirling, from whom I inherited this course. Many thanks to Jonathan Reeve of Tempus Publishing for agreeing to this enjoyable format and to Dr Richard Oram for permission to reproduce some of his library of images. Miss Amanda Beam, currently beginning a study of the Balliol dynasty, also allowed me very kindly to reproduce one of her photographs from a research trip to France: our thesis supervision conversations have already produced some very interesting ideas about the period which I look forward to seeing in print. The staff of the university Library at Stirling were extremely helpful as always. A big thank you must also go to several of my colleagues who tolerated me and cheered me up while I wrote this book at the same time as working (still!) on a monograph on David II of Scotland: Bob McKean, Helen Dingwall, Jim Smyth and Fay Oliver, Iain Hutchinson, George Peden, Colin Nicholson, Emma Macleod (and Tom!), Mike and Helen Rapport, Annabelle Hopkins and Linda Bradley. Finally, thanks as ever to my folks and Ange.

Stirling, July 2002

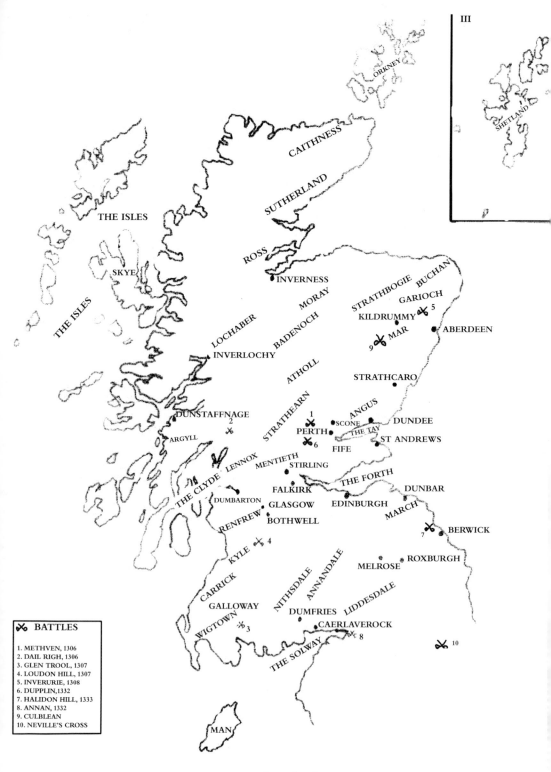

Map of Scotland.

III

ORKNEY

SHETLAND

CAITHNESS

SUTHERLAND

THE ISLES

ROSS

SKYE

INVERNESS

THE ISLES

MORAY

STRATHBOGIE BUCHAN

GARIOCH

KILDRUMMY 5

LOCHABER

BADENOCH

MAR 9

ABERDEEN

INVERLOCHY

ATHOLL

STRATHCARO

DUNSTAFFNAGE

STRATHEARN

2

ANGUS

1

SCONE

DUNDEE

ARGYLL

PERTH

6

THE TAY

FIFE

ST ANDREWS

THE CLYDE

LENNOX

MENTIETH

STIRLING

FALKIRK

THE FORTH

DUNBAR

DUMBARTON

GLASGOW

EDINBURGH

MARCH

RENFREW

BOTHWELL

7

BERWICK

KYLE 4

MELROSE

ROXBURGH

CARRICK

NITHSDALE

ANNANDALE

LIDDESDALE

GALLOWAY

DUMFRIES

WIGTOWN 3

CAERLAVEROCK

8

10

THE SOLWAY

MAN

BATTLES

1. METHVEN, 1306
2. DAIL RIGH, 1306
3. GLEN TROOL, 1307
4. LOUDON HILL, 1307
5. INVERURIE, 1308
6. DUPPLIN, 1332
7. HALIDON HILL, 1333
8. ANNAN, 1332
9. CULBLEAN
10. NEVILLE'S CROSS

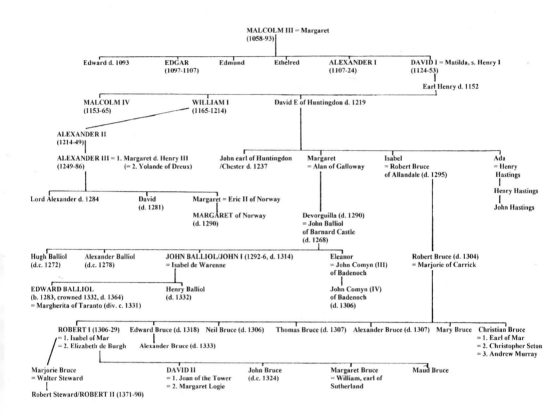

MALCOLM III = Margaret
(1058-93)

Edward d. 1093　　EDGAR　　Edmund　　Ethelred　　ALEXANDER I　　DAVID I = Matilda, s. Henry I
　　　　　　　　(1097-1107)　　　　　　　　　　　　(1107-24)　　(1124-53)

Earl Henry d. 1152

MALCOLM IV　　　　WILLIAM I　　　David E of Huntingdon d. 1219
(1153-65)　　　　　　(1165-1214)

ALEXANDER II
(1214-49)

ALEXANDER III = 1. Margaret d. Henry III　　John earl of Huntingdon　　Margaret　　Isabel　　Ada
(1249-86)　　　(= 2. Yolande of Dreux)　　/Chester d. 1237　　= Alan of Galloway　　= Robert Bruce　　= Henry
　　　　　　　　　　　　　　　　　　　　　　　　　　　　　　　　　　　　　　　of Allandale (d. 1295)　　Hastings

Henry Hastings

Lord Alexander d. 1284　　David　　Margaret = Eric II of Norway　　　　　　　　　　　　　　　　　John Hastings
　　　　　　　　　　　　　(d. 1281)

MARGARET of Norway　　Devorguilla (d. 1290)
(d. 1290)　　　　　　　　= John Balliol
　　　　　　　　　　　　　of Barnard Castle
　　　　　　　　　　　　　(d. 1268)

Hugh Balliol　　Alexander Balliol　　JOHN BALLIOL/JOHN I (1292-6, d. 1314)　　Eleanor　　Robert Bruce (d. 1304)
(d.c. 1272)　　(d.c. 1278)　　　　= Isabel de Warenne　　　　　　　　= John Comyn (III)　　= Marjorie of Carrick
　　　　　　　　　　　　　　　　　　　　　　　　　　　　　　　　　of Badenoch

EDWARD BALLIOL　　　　　　Henry Balliol　　　　　　John Comyn (IV)
(b. 1283, crowned 1332, d. 1364)　(d. 1332)　　　　　　of Badenoch
= Margherita of Taranto (div. c. 1331)　　　　　　　　(d. 1306)

ROBERT I (1306-29)　Edward Bruce (d. 1318)　Neil Bruce (d. 1306)　Thomas Bruce (d. 1307)　Alexander Bruce (d. 1307)　Mary Bruce　Christian Bruce
= 1. Isabel of Mar　　= 1. Earl of Mar
= 2. Elizabeth de Burgh　　Alexander Bruce (d. 1333)　　　　　　　　　　　　　　　　　　　　　　= 2. Christopher Seton
　　　= 3. Andrew Murray

Marjorie Bruce　　　　　　DAVID II　　　　John Bruce　　Margaret Bruce　　Maud Bruce
= Walter Steward　　　　= 1. Joan of the Tower　(d.c. 1324)　= William, earl of
　　　　　　　　　　　= 2. Margaret Logie　　　　　　　Sutherland
Robert Steward/ROBERT II (1371-90)

The Royal Succession.

INTRODUCTION: FAMILIES AT WAR

In August 1299, an English spy reported news of a Scottish council of war to his King, Edward I. It was just over a year since the Scots' inspiring if unexpected leader, William Wallace, the second son of a minor knight, had been defeated by Edward at the battle of Falkirk. But the Scots had continued to rebel. In the intervening twelve months two major noblemen had emerged to act as 'Guardians of the realm' to lead the fight in the name of their absent King, John I (or John Balliol), then a prisoner in the Tower of London. However, these new generals – Robert Bruce, Earl of Carrick, and John Comyn, son of the Lord of Badenoch – were ill-matched allies.

Both in their twenties, these two ambitious knights were now the active representatives in the kingdom of the most powerful families on either side of an intense dynastic competition for the Scottish throne. Comyn and his cousin, the Earl of Buchan, and their extensive family backed the right to be king of John Balliol (Badenoch's uncle); but Bruce was always on the look out for the chance to push the claim of his own kindred, the Bruces of Annandale. As such, the outcome relayed by Edward I's agent in 1299, as a witness to the war council held at Peebles at the height of the campaigning season, was perhaps predictable.

William Wallace, it was reported, had left the kingdom on some unexplained mission to the continent without the permission of the two Guardians. As a result, one of Comyn's followers, Sir David Graham, laid claim to Wallace's lands and goods. But his demand was opposed by Wallace's brother, Malcolm, whom we are told was an adherent of Robert Bruce. A blazing row ensued. In the resulting scuffle 'John Comyn leaped at the earl of Carrick and seized him by the throat, and the earl of Buchan turned on the bishop of St Andrews'. In the end, it took the calming influence of more neutral nobles, like James the Steward, to part the factions: then, shortly before they all went their separate ways, the Bishop of St Andrews was appointed as Chief-Guardian over and above Comyn and Bruce.

Here at once is graphic proof of the violent personal and political conflict which threatened to tear the Scottish community apart at the dawn of the fourteenth century, exposing it fatally to English imperialism. In order to assert their claim to power in Scotland, landed nobles like Balliol, the Comyns and Bruce were forced to consider breaking violently with the tradition of holding lands in both the Scottish and English kingdoms (and very often in Ireland too). In doing so these men would be forfeited by Edward I and cease to be part of the wider feudal aristocracy with connections throughout the British Isles. They would become simply Scottish king and lords: big fish in a small pond. Yet to achieve this, one party would not only have to fight off English claims of overlordship but it would also have to wrap itself up in a flag of wartime patriotism so as to vilify and destroy the rival claimant and his followers in Scotland. This losing party would turn naturally to aid from its feudal lord, the king of England, who would be only too glad to exploit such a 'fifth column' to make Scotland a vassal state.

This dilemma of whether or not to sacrifice valuable lands in England for unchallenged power in the northern kingdom (or try and retain both) would cause the chiefs and scions of many of the Scottish realm's leading families to vacillate, rebel, submit and betray by turns over the course of two generations. As might be expected, and as one contemporary English chronicler put it,

'in all this fighting the Scots were so divided that often a father was with the Scots and his son with the

English, or one brother was with the Scots and another with the English, or even one individual was first on one side and then on the other'.

As we shall see, this quandry of identity and loyalty was present most dramatically in the early career of Robert Bruce, Earl of Carrick, the man who would be king after 1306. However, for all the big players of the realm and more minor figures (like Sir David Graham) this conflict more immediately created opportunities and dangers at a local level. In many ways, the Bruce v. Balliol struggle was a regional feud in south-west Scotland writ large. The Bruces as Lords of Annandale and Earls of Carrick clashed with their immediate neighbour, John Balliol, Lord of Galloway, and his in-laws, the Comyns, sheriffs of Wigtown and thus leading policemen for the Scottish kings in the south-west throughout the thirteenth century. The widespread family trees of these rival kindreds not only brought them familial claims to the Scottish throne after Alexander III died without leaving a male heir in 1286; but each of these family ties also embroiled their many in-laws and allies throughout the realm in both national and civil war. Neighbour took the chance to destroy neighbour and in the north-east, the western approaches and south-east of Scotland especially we shall see that men most often chose a side in opposition to their local rival.

For others in the kingdom, the cause was arguably much clearer. The leading Scottish churchmen in particular could be said to have already formed a binding national and institutional outlook on relations with England and the Scottish crown before 1286: they had done so in protecting the Scottish Church from English interference throughout the twelfth and thirteenth centuries. Thus after 1286 the bishops would very often sustain the Scottish resistance effort against England – both in war and diplomacy – through its lowest ebbs. The integrity of the Scottish Church depended upon the maintenance of a free Scotland with its own king, owing allegiance to no-one but God and the Pope. Even the great monastic abbeys, priories and nunneries founded by kings of Scots between c.1100 and 1249 as 'daughters' of leading English or French religious houses had some fear of English meddling in their liberties and vast landed resources.

A much more practical, daily choice of loyalties could also be said to have lain before men of lesser rank in Scotland – minor nobles like William Wallace, the townsmen and merchants and the mass of the populace on the land. For such people the Anglo-Scottish conflict could be much more strongly drawn by ethnic differences and was very often a simple choice between oppression in the face of new demands from strangers or relative liberty and customary rights under familiar landlords: put at its most simple, the freedom to make a livelihood. Yet even all these bishops and abbots, lesser knights and esquires, trading burgesses and farming freeholders were often younger sons and kin of the leading noble families of the realm or under their direct feudal influence as their tenants: they were thus just as prone to local rivalries and hatreds, or fear and resolve in the face of war, as the leading laymen of the realm, be they of Anglo-Norman, Gaelic or mixed stock.

Besides, for all of these peoples dwelling in the Scottish kingdom it would above all require a victor in the underlying civil feud – Bruce v. Balliol – and the resulting re-establishment of active adult kingship in Scotland for the realm and all of its estates to survive English attack. Most Scots would have to back a horse that could win and pick a side at some point. This was a violent conflict which would see first blood drawn in 1286 – three years before Edward I's first concerted interference in the fate of the realm. The resulting internal strife in Scotland would then be marked by a bitter struggle for the reins of power, the spectacular murder by Bruce of Comyn of Badenoch in 1306, years of fighting which wasted the Scottish Lowlands and the co-existence of two rival crowned kings of Scots at war in the 1330s. Indeed, far from being settled by the achievements of the hero king, Robert Bruce, by the time of his death in 1329, this struggle would not really end until the resignation of his claim to the Scottish throne by the sad, dejected figure of John I's son, Edward Balliol, to Edward III of England in 1356. The impact of this civil war on the Scottish political landscape was thus in many ways far more important than the struggle with the 'auld enemy'.

PART ONE

THE SCOTTISH SUCCESSION CRISIS

1

KINGS AND NOBLES
BEFORE 1286

'No-one but God alone has the right to the homage for my kingdom of Scotland, and I hold it of no-one except God alone!'

Alexander III to Edward I at
Westminster, 1278.

Before 1237 the MacMalcolm (or Canmore) kings of Scots were the more consistent aggressors in relations between the Scottish and English kingdoms. The kings of England – descended from William, the Norman Conqueror of 1066 – would from the first assume a strong air of superiority over their northern neighbours. But in the late eleventh and twelfth centuries it was the kings of the smaller, poorer and militarily weaker realm of Scotland who were more readily prepared to resort to actual force to expand their influence south at the expense of the geographical extent of the English monarchy's rule.

For their part, the English kings were more generally concerned to secure a peaceful northern border while they attended to more pressing concerns in securing their own southern lands as well as Gascony, Ireland and Wales. Thus when in 1072 Malcolm III of Scotland (1057–93) attempted to seize the county (and old kingdom) of Northumberland at the fringes of William's power, the Norman king invaded Scotland as far north as Abernethy near Perth but only took a personal submission from the king of Scots: he extracted no recognition that Malcolm (and his sons by the Saxon princess, Margaret) would hold Scotland of him as their feudal superior.

This uneasy English containment of Canmore territorial ambition was to be the overlying theme of Anglo-Scottish relations for the next 150 years. In part, though, William the Conqueror and his successors were responsible for further fuelling Malcolm's sons and heirs with the expansionist Anglo-Norman spirit of the age. Malcolm and his eldest son, Edward, were killed invading Northumberland once more in 1093. But his second and fifth sons, Kings Edgar (1097–1107) and Alexander I (1107–24), both required the help of the Norman kings of England to secure their throne against dynastic challenges from within Scotland. A king like Alexander then ruled his realm predominantly from a Gaelic base north of the Forth. Yet in expanding his royal authority to the north, west and south in Scotland he was the first to begin to employ the patronage of monastic orders and knights of Norman stock. These were potent new forces for colonisation and the establishment of political power then spreading across north-western Europe. Malcolm III's sons had been educated in such ways as English 'guests' after 1072: Alexander was thus also a son-in-law of King Henry I of England and helped in his Welsh wars.

But it was Alexander's younger brother and heir, David, who really drove home this form of 'hybrid' expansionist monarchy in Scotland. Indeed by the time of his accession to the Scottish throne in 1124 David was a leading figure in the English kingdom: a brother-in-law of Henry I, a sheriff and justiciar, Earl of Northumbria by right of his wife as well as lord of the valuable, honour of Huntingdon in the English Midlands and other lands. With Henry's backing (in intimidating Alexander) David had already begun to expand his influence and the lordship of his own Anglo-Norman followers into Tweeddale, Teviotdale, the Lothians and the rest of southern Scotland before 1124. Once king of Scots,

David pushed the extension of the royal writ throughout his realm on the back of the plantation of many great monastic houses, the consolidation of royal trading burghs and landed patronage to ambitious Anglo-Norman families who had first served him in northern England: kindreds like the Bruces, Morevilles, Stewarts, Murrays, Comyns and de Soules to name but a few. By the close of his reign David had thus overseen the expansion of such feudal tenure – in which nobles held land of the crown in return for specified military service – into Fife, Moray, Clydeside and parts of the south-west. He had also established a system of royal household government based on the English model as well as a judicial network of sheriffdoms and justiciars throughout the Lowland localities; a rationalised Church system of bishoprics and parishes had also helped expand the frontier of Canmore power in tandem with the creeping spread of abbeys, priories and nunneries. Many of the existing Gaelic tenantry of the realm were either keen or forced to buy into this hierarchic way of life of king, knight, castle, bishop, burgess and freeholder.

1. The Seal of Alexander III (1249–86)
Stable Scottish kingship: on one side, the king sits enthroned on the stone of Scone dispensing justice and patronage to nobles, Church and burghs; on the other, the king as leader in war.

However, the competitive and charismatic David was not above turning his blend of Scottish and Anglo-Norman kingship against his former English patrons when an opportunity arose: this was the nature of the beast of medieval monarchy. As king, David had inherited a number of Anglo-Scottish flashpoints from Alexander I in addition to the debatable positioning of the border. There had been repeated attempts by the archbishoprics of Canterbury and York to assert control over the Scottish Church: this had been allied to English kings' obstruction of Canmore appeals to the Popes to be granted the rite of a full coronation and unction with holy oil for their dynasty. All this can only have added to David's intolerance for the implicit and inferior 'client' status of the Scottish kingdom in relation to England. But when he was denied the right to retain his earldom of Northumbria after the death of his English wife David was pushed too far.

Thus when the troubled King Stephen acceded the English throne in 1135 David took advantage of the ensuing civil war to attempt to annex with force the three northern English counties, Northumberland, Cumberland and Westmorland. Despite a heavy defeat in the battle of the Standard in 1138, David was largely successful as England succumbed to inner turmoil. When he died in 1153 David would be based at Carlisle and allowed to hold much of the northern counties as a feudal vassal of the victor over Stephen, Henry II: David had also secured Tynedale and Newcastle. Back home, David's regime had at the same time resisted revolts by dynastic rivals from within Scotland in the outlying zones of the far north and south-west: the right of succession by primogeniture (through the nearest male issue of the king) had also been consolidated when David's grandson, Malcolm, had been paraded around the kingdom in 1152 by the most important of the ancient native Scottish earls, Fife, the lord responsible for placing any new king on the stone of Scone for his inauguration.

However, in an age of intense personal monarchy – when the fortunes of a realm were heavily dependent upon the force of character of their king – fate soon swung against the Scottish realm. Malcolm IV (1153–65) was much less able to stand up to the hard-headed kingship of Henry II. Not only did Henry deprive this king of Scots of Northumbria but he insisted upon Malcolm – and some of those lords of Norman descent in Scotland who also held lands in the southern realm – doing military service against the French. Upon his return from the continent Malcolm faced rebellion in several quarters not only from dynastic opponents in the south-west and western isles but also from Scottish tenants-in-chief who resented his subservience to England even though he only did homage for his English lands. There was a strong perception – even in England – that Scotland's kings of the late twelfth century:

> 'profess themselves to be rather Frenchmen in race, manners and language and outlook; and after reducing the Scots to utter servitude they admit only Frenchmen to their friendship and service'.

It would indeed take a shocking scare in his dealings with Anglo-Norman England before Malcolm's brother and heir, William I (1165–1214), turned to focus on the consolidation of royal and feudal authority in northern and south-western Scotland.

William (later known as the Lion) began his reign determined to recover Northumbria. When offers to aid Henry II against the French in exchange for this county failed William resorted to force. He allied with Louis VII of France and Henry's rebellious heir to attack the English monarch in return for the coveted lands. But this shrewd policy met with disaster on the battlefield. At Alnwick in July 1174 William was captured and led to the Tower of London with his feet bound beneath his horse (a fate which would also befall Robert Bruce's heir, David II, in 1346). Now Henry II sought to alter radically the vague Anglo-Scottish relationship in his favour. Under the terms of the treaty of Falaise of December 1174 William and his heirs were obliged to give homage to Henry and his heirs 'for Scotland and all of his other lands'. William's subjects were also to do homage to the English crown, if need be for both their Scottish and English lands: the English claim that this had always been the 'custom' between the two realms was a liberty of the victor-in-arms.

In reality, though, what Henry II wanted was to use this stick to keep the Scots neutral while he solved his own domestic problems. Thus when Richard I came to the English throne in July 1189 and quickly announced his intention to go on crusade William was able to buy out his humiliating submission of overlordship (at a cost of 10,000 merks, at least two years' income). This 'Quitclaim of Canterbury' was a reassertion of independence consolidated in 1192 by recognition for the Scottish Church as a 'special daughter' of the Pope in Rome and thus exempt from English ecclesiastical authority. These landmark documents undoubtedly contributed to the stirring of a strong collective identity binding together Scotland's Crown, Church elite and, increasingly, its landed nobility. This was a sense of belonging which would lead to the elevation of both St Andrew and Malcolm III's wife, Margaret, as national saints by the mid-thirteenth century.

But this was also a nascent sense of national sovereignty which would spur William on to recover Northumbria once more after 1200. However, in attempting to exploit the internal strife of the reign of John I of England William nearly came unstuck again: faced down by John on more than one occasion towards the end of his reign William had to give up his hopes of holding extensive northern English lands and concede more money, hostages and control of his heirs' marriages so as to secure his neighbour's goodwill and avoid a revival of the homage question.

Yet fate's pendulum soon swung the other way. The much tougher and cannier Alexander II of Scotland (1214–49) was able to take advantage of the Magna Carta crisis of John's last years: by allying with the French and English barons he seemed set to claim all of the northern counties just as he had occupied Carlisle. The accession of Henry III, however, denied him his triumph. By 1217, in fact, Alexander had been obliged to admit the reality that his English holdings would be limited to Tynedale and Huntingdon (the latter to be held by his cousin, John, Earl of Chester). Anglo-Scottish relations now entered into the prolonged period of relative amity which would still exist in 1286. Alexander II married Henry's sister at York in 1220. This Canmore king and his son and heir would thus turn their energies instead to expanding their authority within what are now known as Scotland's borders, concentrating on over-awing the autonomous lordship of Galloway (by 1234) and the Western Isles (nominally under Norse rule).

Nonetheless, there were moments of considerable Anglo-Scottish tension ahead. When John of Chester died in 1237 Alexander II reacted to the loss of Huntingdon by going to the brink of war: the treaty of York that year codified the rough casting of the Anglo-Scottish border at the Solway-Tweed line but there was a further stand-off in 1244 as the English continued to invoke the language of Falaise in dealings with Scotland and Rome. However, the fact that various contemporary chronicles reported that both the English and the Scots were 'right blithe [glad] of that accordance' when peace was reaffirmed in 1244 underlines the reality that by the mid-century these two expansionist monarchies and their realms were closely bound together both by a shared faith and aristocratic culture as well as by the more practical bonds of extensive cross-border landholding by noble families, monastic houses and their respective royal dynasties who, like their nobles, continued to inter-marry.

Thus when Alexander III (1249–86) came to throne as a minor there was no great apprehension amongst Scotland's chief nobles and churchmen that Henry III should have considerable influence over the northern kingdom following the marriage of the boy-king to his daughter, Margaret, in 1251. Henry did make an attempt to extract a concession of English feudal superiority over Scotland from his new son-in-law. But this was quickly side-stepped by the Scots who, split into two factions – centered around the Durwards and Comyns – were quite happy to compete for political power and territory in Scotland by calling in turn for the intervention of Henry in the Scottish council.

But after enduring two such English-engineered coups in Scotland, Alexander III emerged as very much his own man by 1260. Unconcerned, as yet, to reopen the issue of the northern English counties, Alexander concentrated on the Western Isles, securing their sovereignty in 1266 after a Norse invasion was thwarted at Largs in 1263. He also provided amply for the Canmore succession, siring two sons and a daughter with Margaret by the 1270s, children for whom good marriages were found on the continent. Scottish lords with English lands were permitted to aid Henry III in his civil wars in 1264 and joined his sons on crusade in 1270–2.

Yet with the accession of Edward I in 1272 a much more subtle, uncertain Anglo-Scottish game was initiated. In 1278, Edward I re-opened the issue of overlordship for Scotland in an exchange in a Westminster parliament (where Alexander had appeared to do homage for his English lands of Tynedale). The record of this confrontation was censored by both sides during the wars of the 1290s. According to English sources, Edward reserved his right to return to the matter again in the future: but the Scots would recall that Alexander (quoted above) had resisted this unfounded demand boldly. The matter was dropped. But for many historians this was the first clear sign that Edward – ever the opportunist – had an eye to expand his empire northwards now that the English lands on the continent had been reduced by the French.

Alexander III, too, was aware of such English possibilities and could not afford to alienate his brother-in-law. Thus when calamity was heaped upon calamity and all of Alexander's children by Margaret (who had died in 1275) had in turn perished by January 1284, the Scottish king sought at once to pander to and guard against Edward's interest. Alexander summoned a parliament of his nobles and prelates in February 1284 which he caused to recognise the right of his grand-daughter, Margaret, daughter of Eric II of Norway, as heir to his throne. Then, at the close of April that year, Alexander replied to a letter of condolence from Edward I, writing that because 'we are united together perpetually God willing, by the tie of indissoluble affection... much good may come to pass yet through your kinswoman', this Maid of Norway: the Scots king was perhaps hinting at the possibility of a marriage between the Maid and a son of Edward who would then go on to become monarch of Scotland should Alexander fail to have another son. But to provide for the latter eventuality (the king was only in his forties) Alexander also took another wife, following his father by marrying a French woman, Yolande of Dreux, as his second queen. It was this young consort whom he was on his way to visit on a stormy night in March 1286 when Alexander was thrown from his horse and killed tragically near Kinghorn in Fife.

It is, then, this complex background of ostensibly friendly Anglo-Scottish relations before 1286 – though perhaps with escalating English interest in the thorny question of overlordship – into which many historians have attempted to weave a dramatic story of long-term Bruce v. Balliol hatred rooted in an ancient rivalry. This historical myth was based in part upon the fact that by the late thirteenth century the Bruces and Balliols had married the Carrick and Galloway descendants respectively of the feuding offspring of Fergus, lord of Galloway (d.1161). Yet in truth these two immigrant kindreds of Bruce and Balliol on the whole followed separate if similar (and, perhaps, even at times amicable) paths of lordship between both kingdoms. If there was any conscious rivalry between these two houses and their potential supporters before Alexander III's demise it emerged only latterly through the accidents of marriage, birth and death.

The family of de Brus (Bruce) hailed originally from Normandy but with holdings in Yorkshire, Durham and Cumberland by 1124 they were natural agents for David I to plant in the lordship of Annandale (in return for five knights' service). This made the Bruces a chivalric buffer for the Canmores in policing the troublesome south-west. That said, their English lands often caused the family to side against Scottish kings intent on seizing the northern English counties. In 1135–8 the Bruce family chief (and the Balliols) supported Stephen in the face of David I's incursions: the younger Bruce heir backed the Scottish king. But all the Bruces opposed William I's attacks in 1173–4 and briefly lost their Scottish lands. In sum, despite their large Scottish holdings the Bruces were not unequivocally 'Scottish' or pro-Canmore in outlook and did not occupy a major office in that realm by the turn of the century.

In contrast, the Balliols were much later additions to the Scottish political landscape. Originally from Picardy (where they retained lands into the fourteenth century) by c.1124 they were lords of Barnard Castle in Yorkshire, Bywell in Northumberland and other lands in Durham and elsewhere. But the future royal house of Balliol did not receive favour in Scotland from David I: they really remained English magnates (occupying sheriff's offices in northern England). Thus throughout the Scottish incursions of c.1135–1217 the Balliols held loyal to England, including in 1216 when Alexander II targeted Barnard Castle.

In fact, this Balliol branch did not come into substantial Scottish estates until 1233 when John (I) Balliol married Devorguilla, third daughter of Alan, Lord of Galloway (d.1234), and his wife, Margaret, eldest daughter of David, Earl of Huntingdon and Lord of Garioch (d.1219), the brother of King William I of Scotland. The death in 1237 of Devorguilla's uncle (on her mother's side), John, Earl of Chester and Lord of Huntingdon, brought this John Balliol many more lands through his wife, namely a third of the former lands of the Scottish Crown in England (in Bedfordshire, Buckinghamshire,

Cambridgeshire, Huntingdonshire, Leicestershire, Lincolnshire, Northamptonshire, Rutland and Middlesex) as well as some significant Scottish territories like a share of the north-east lordship of Garioch. But in 1237 a neighbouring third of these lordships also went – with little apparent controversy – to the fifth Robert Bruce of Annandale whose father had married the second daughter of David, Earl of Huntingdon. The remaining third went to the family of Earl David's third daughter's husband, Henry de Hastings.

With their inheritance in 1237 of these former Scottish Crown lands by right of their marriages into the royal line of Earl David it might have been expected that the Bruces' and Balliols' interest in Scotland would have grown. There is evidence that this did happen. It was in 1238 that Robert Bruce of Annandale would later claim that he was named by a Scottish parliament as heir presumptive to the throne of the as-yet childless Alexander II (just before a campaign to the Western Isles) because he (Bruce, born about 1220) was the eldest living child of Earl David's daughters. Then during Alexander III's minority, Bruce seems to have backed the Durward party in challenging the Comyns and their supporters for power over the infant king. In 1251, however, the Comyns' appeal to Henry III heralded the introduction of Robert de Ros of Wark and John (I) Balliol of Barnard Castle as guardians of the young royal couple acting in Henry's interest while the Comyns swept the Durward supporters from government (until a counter-coup in 1255).

However, although Bruce of Annandale and Balliol might thus be said to have joined opposite sides of this factionalism they displayed no animosity for each other as territorial neighbours nor any awareness of their potentially royal role. If there was any early thirteenth-century tension in Scotland which did intensify after 1251 it was caused by the opposition of Bruce and many others to the growing Comyn establishment in Scotland. Another Anglo-Norman family introduced by David I, the Comyns had emerged as the first incomer earls in Scotland as holders of Buchan by 1212: their acquisition of the northern lordship of Badenoch and roles as justiciars of Scotia and Galloway (and sheriffs of Wigtown) made them a leading political force. By the 1270s the Comyns' marriage connections confirmed their backing by the kindreds of the Dunbar Earls of March, the Earls of Strathearn, the Umphraville Earls of

2. Marjorie, heiress of the earldom of Carrick, 'kidnaps' and marries Robert Bruce
According to tradition, this Bruce, father of the man who would be king, was on
his way home from a crusade during which Majorie's father had been killed; their
marriage would further elevate the Bruces' influence in Scotland a decade before
Alexander III's death.

Angus, the Earls of Fife and the kindreds of Brechin, Soules, Lindsay, Balliol, Siward, Mowbray, Macdougall, Murray and many others. However, in the 1250s several of these nobles had sided with Bruce in backing Alan Durward (who died in 1268, the same year as John (I) Balliol). Therefore no long-term factionalism leading directly to the succession crisis and civil war of post-March 1286 should necessarily be read into this minority period of 1249–60.

In fact, it can be argued that after a compromise council was agreed for Alexander III in 1258, the Comyns, Bruces and Balliols returned to their roles as Anglo-Scottish nobles, continuing to operate without contradiction by holding lands in both realms. In this aristocratic circle these kindreds could even be comrades-in-arms, supporting Henry III and his heir at Lewes against English rebels in 1264. In 1270–2, Bruce, Eustace and Hugh Balliol (sons of John (I)) and others of their kin, accompanied Adam, Earl of Carrick, and a number of other Scots knights on crusade to the Holy Land with Henry's sons Edmund and Edward. Balliol's widow, meanwhile, consolidated his foundation of Balliol College in Oxford. Both the Balliols, Bruces and, to a lesser extent, the Comyns, kept substantial houses in London to be near the English court, in addition to their many English manors. It would be premature, too, to suggest that with his son Robert's marriage in 1272 to the heiress of Carrick, Robert of Annandale became increasingly aware of any growing or natural rivalry with his Comyn and Balliol neighbours in south-west Scotland. Like John (II) Balliol, the third son of Devorguilla and her heir presumptive by 1278 (the future king of Scots), Bruce of Annandale probably retained a stronger interest in his affairs in England where his son was keeper of Carlisle. Neither family acquired any significant office in Scotland before 1286, although the descendants of a junior line of the Balliol kindred (those of Urr in Galloway and Inverkeilor in Angus) did sometimes act as chamberlain for Alexander III.

However, when King Alexander's immediate family began to die off between 1275 and 1284 the atmosphere may have changed. It is tempting to speculate that John (II) Balliol (born about 1248–50), heir presumptive to his mother's Scottish lands after the deaths of his elder brothers, gave up his studies for the Church at Durham about 1278 and looked to safeguard his estates and the outside chance of his succession to the throne. While his elder

3. Monument to Alexander III, Kinghorn, Fife
Alexander's body was found on the shore near here after he had
perished riding through a stormy night in March 1286 to see his new
French bride: Scotland's succession crisis ensued.

brothers had been named Hugh, Alan (and, perhaps, Alexander), John named his own children Edward (born 1283) and Henry, displaying a close affiliation with royal English blood. He may have been influenced to do so not only by his in-laws the Comyns, who must have had one eye by now on securing their power in Scotland in the event of the male Canmores' extinction: but Balliol may also have begun to act more and more *c.*1283–6 on the advice of his father-in-law, John de Warenne, Earl of Surrey, whose daughter, Isabel, he had wed about February 1281.

If this was so, then it is likely that the Bruces of Annandale and Carrick, too, must have become increasingly aware – after the deaths of Alexander III's second son, David, in 1281, then his daughter in 1283 and finally Prince Alexander, the king's eldest son, in January 1284 – that a royal destiny might be beckoning. The fact that the Bruces' chief rivals in such a contested succession would be their immediate neighbours in south-west Scotland must now have come into play. The several sons of Robert Bruce and Marjorie of Carrick were brought up with strong local connections as well as experience on the national stage: Robert Bruce (the future king, born 1274) would spend some time as a young man in the English royal household but he would also be fostered out in the Carrick tradition to a Gaelic south-west or Irish family, the kind of lords to whom the Bruces would turn for support in challenging for the kingship after 1286. Was a growing sense of rivalry with the Balliols also the reason why another brother, Alexander Bruce, would study for the Church at Cambridge and not Oxford?

Alexander III himself had clearly attempted to guard against such in-fighting over his throne. The Parliamentary Act of February 1284 recognising the Maid of Norway's right of succession significantly bound over all his subjects to obey this statute on pain of censure by the Scottish Church and military action by the nobility. But when the worst case scenario did transpire at the foot of storm-lashed cliffs in Fife in 1286 this piece of paper and oath would not be enough to prevent the Scottish political community from being riven by divisions far more intense than those of the 1250s. This Bruce v. Balliol/Comyn civil conflict would be just what the predatory Edward I of England would need to intrude his overlordship.

2

THE INTERREGNUM AND
GREAT CAUSE, 1286–92

'Quhen Alexander the king wes deid,
That Scotland had to steyr and leid,
The land sex yer and mayr perfay
Lay desolat eftyr hys day
Till that the baronage at the last
Assemblyt thaim and fayndyt fast
To cheys a king thar land to ster
That off auncestry cummyn wer
Off kingis that aucht that reawté
And mayst had rycht thair king to be'.

John Barbour, *The Bruce*, *c*.1371–5

The late king's fears about rivalry between his nobles in the event
of his death without a son quickly proved all too well-founded. At
a parliament in Scone in April 1286 there was 'a bitter pleading
regarding the right of succession to the kingdom' between Robert
Bruce of Annandale and John Balliol. Despite Alexander's

insistence in 1284 that his significant subjects swear an oath to recognise 'the illustrious girl, Margaret... as our lady and rightful heir of our lord king of Scotland', it is likely that most of the nobles and prelates already had their eye on who the Maid of Norway would wed. The 1286 assembly thus gave an ambivalent oath instead to 'the nearest by blood by right who will inherit': the Bruces, John Balliol, the Comyns and others might now offer up their own sons as a match to be king.

However, the rancour of this debate in parliament may also have been intensified by a two-fold Bruce reaction: first of all against the very notion that a mere foreign girl should be queen by insisting instead that the kingship should go to the nearest adult male heirs with Bruce, of course, taken ahead of Balliol; but secondly a backlash against the Comyns' continued monopoly of royal government.

For the 1286 parliament also elected six Guardians in the name of the 'community of the realm'. Yet far from being the result of a genuine vote and a representative cross-section of all the political and regional interests in the kingdom in its choice of two earls, two barons and two bishops, this administration was driven by the Comyn establishment to the deliberate (and perhaps physical) exclusion of the Bruces. Alexander Comyn, Earl of Buchan, and John (II), Lord of Badenoch, were both Guardians along with the leading churchmen of the realm, Robert Wishart, Bishop of Glasgow, and William Fraser, Bishop of St Andrews. But the other Guardian Earl, Duncan of Fife, had marital and landed connections to the Comyns as did the families of the Dunbar Earls of March, the Earls of Strathearn, the Macdougalls of Argyll, the Umphraville Earls of Angus, Soules of Liddesdale, Brechin of Barclay, the Frasers, Murrays and Sinclairs and, of course, Balliol: these houses filled most of the sheriffships, justiciarships and other offices of the realm after 1286 while a Comyn was Chamberlain. The final guardian, James (the) Steward – later a Bruce supporter along with Bishop Wishart – would be loyal to this Comyn administration while it lasted.

In securing such control the Comyns were undoubtedly aided by their pedigree in government since the 1250s. But they may also have already been boosted by the fact that most significant Scots recognised that if a male claim to the throne (or for Margaret's hand) needed to be backed then that of John Balliol – the brother-in-law of Badenoch – had the greatest legal weight. All of this proved too

4. Seal of the Scottish Guardians, 1286–92.
On one side the royal arms, on the other the cross of St Andrew and the legend
St Andrew as the leader of the compatriot Scots.

much to the Robert Bruces of Annandale and Carrick. Their anger may have been stayed until a pregnancy claimed by Alexander III's widow, Yolande, proved to be phantom. But in autumn 1286 the Bruce father and son and their landed following struck out at their perceived opponents, attacking the Balliol lordship of Buittle and attempting to take the royal castles of Dumfries and Wigtown where the Comyns were sheriffs: they also interfered in the Balliol and Hastings' holdings in the valuable lordship of Garioch.

This regional conflict probably rumbled on for many months. Surviving records from this period are extremely sketchy but the Guardians' accounts for 1288–90 reveal that much of the south-west had been waste for over two years. Moreover, the potential for this violence to spiral on to the national stage must have been very real. Extra guards and defence works were paid for at Edinburgh Castle where there was a prolonged 'danger of war': Stirling Castle, too, was manned in readiness. Moreover, the Bruces' ability to rouse significant opposition to Comyn dominance should not be underestimated. The famous 'Turnberry band', sealed in September 1286 by the Bruce lords in conjunction with James Steward, Walter Stewart, Earl of Menteith, Patrick Dunbar, Earl of March, and Angus MacDonald of Islay may ostensibly have been a declaration of support from men with west-coast interests to aid the Earls of Ulster; but it may also have spoken to potential territorial rivals of the Comyns and their allies. It was, at least, an oath of service by these lords:

31

'reserving our faith to the lord king of England and to whoever, by reason of his blood relationship to Lord Alexander, late king of Scotland... shall be given and be put in possession of the kingdom of Scotland',

as if that power were up for grabs.

By 1289, though, the impression given is of one of the Guardians' general ability to contain the Bruces. Even James Steward seems to have complied in mobilising the tenantry of the abbey of Melrose to help police the men of Annandale and Carrick. Yet in reality the Bruces may have been able to sustain their pressure and intrude their interests through appeals to Edward I. It had probably been the Comyns who had first sought friendly advice from their former crusading companion the English king in late spring and summer 1286. Then on a campaign of conquest in France, Edward nonetheless enjoyed a strong reputation throughout Europe as a statesman and arbitrator. The Comyns, besides, must have had strong memories from the 1250s of the advantages to be gained through soliciting backing from a strong English king in facing down political challenges in Scotland during a royal minority. Crucially, however, although too busy to reply in 1286, by 1288–9 Edward must have sensed a golden opportunity to intrude his influence into Scotland by exploiting both the marital status of his grand-niece, the Maid of Norway, and the yawning divisions erupting amongst the Scots, many of whom held lands of him in England.

Thus it was perhaps either through Edward I's insistence – or by means of armed force and growing support amongst the Scottish political community – that by October 1289 Robert Bruce the elder of Annandale had been allowed to join a Scottish embassy to Norway: he accompanied Bishops Wishart and Fraser and Comyn of Badenoch. That the Comyn party was in no position to prevent Bruce's input is suggested by the regime's inability to replace two of its number as Guardians: Duncan, Earl of Fife, who was murdered by a local rival about 1288; and Alexander, Earl of Buchan, the most experienced Comyn politico, who had died by autumn 1289.

Opposite Page: 5. John Balliol, Edward I, Robert Bruce of Annandale (the Old Competitor) and the Maid of Norway.
Once the Maid died in autumn 1290 all the serious money was on Balliol (backed by the Comyns) to become king. Nonetheless, the process of the 'Great Cause' under Edward I still took almost two years.

Once off the boat at Bergen in Norway, there is evidence to suggest that the Scottish envoys may have sought to forward their own noble scions as potential husbands for the Maid. If John Balliol or either of his sons, Edward (born 1283) or Henry, were not suitable then the Comyns might even offer one of their own; the Bruces could of course present the youngest Robert Bruce, the man who would be king (born 1274), or one of his several brothers. That the Bruces were interested in marriage alliances is underlined by the match in 1293 of the younger Robert's aunt, Isabella, to the widower King Eric of Norway himself. In 1289, then, it may have been only Edward I who was committed to the idea – hinted at by Alexander III in 1284 – of the Maid wedding his five-year-old son and heir, Edward.

The Comyns and their party would surely have been glad to facilitate this match and to use Edward I's influence as a means of bolstering their governance of Scotland. But the wily English monarch was determined to present the Scots with a *fait accompli*. Sweetening the troubled young Norwegian king with cash Edward also secured in secret, by May 1289, a papal dispensation for his son to marry the Maid long before talks had reached a climax. Indeed, the first indenture concluded between the Scots, Norway and Edward in England was a mere preliminary. That said, this treaty of Salisbury of 9 November 1289 does point to the bubbling factionalism within Scotland. Under its terms Eric was to send his daughter to England or Scotland 'free and quit of all contract of marriage and betrothal', hinting at mutual Scottish and English fears about private deals. Edward I for his part would also send Margaret north unwed if she first came to his realm: nor would the Scots marry her off without her father's say-so. But most significant of all, Margaret was only to arrive to be made queen 'when the kingdom is settled and at peace': factional violence was clearly still an issue.

While marriage of the Maid to Prince Edward may thus have become the only way for the Scots to avoid a civil war, the Guardians and community were not so naïve as to let the English king simply take over and absorb the independent kingdom which would soon pass to his son and heir. Although the Scots agreed in March 1290 to go ahead with the marriage (as news of the papal dispensation broke) alarm bells were clearly rung by Edward's interference that summer in the Isle of Man and his appointment of Bishop Bek of Durham to oversee both the Scottish Crown's lands in northern England and the imminent newly-weds' interests in Scotland. In the final negotiations for the betrothal the Scots – with the lead surely taken by churchmen – were on their guard to protect Scottish independence under regnal union.

The resulting treaty of Birgham of 18 July 1290 contained many now famous clauses designed to guarantee the integrity of Scotland's Church, parliament, laws and customs: there was to be no question of homage by the Scots for their northern lands or realm to Prince Edward when he became king of England – he would be crowned distinctly as king of Scots and administer that kingdom's affairs in Scotland with the advice of Scottish officers. Moreover, even the Bruces and the Comyns could be united in seeking the guarantee that they would not be required to do military service for their Scottish lands in English armies or pay unfamiliar, English-style taxes.

Just how in practice this piece of paper would prevent an English king consort of Scotland – controlled by a father skilful in the law – from imposing whatever rule he saw fit was surely a fatal omission. But it was never put to the test. After King Eric had declined Edward I's suspicious attempts to bring the Maid to England in English ships, the poor girl set out for Scotland in autumn 1290. She died just before reaching Orkney and an audience with envoys sent by Bishop Fraser of St Andrews. That this prelate had been concerned to oversee the conclusion of a deal which would secure the Comyn party in government is suggested by letters sent to Edward I as news of the Maid's death broke. It was this second tragic royal death which now heralded the eruption of rival campaigns in Scotland to secure the throne.

For on 7 October 1290 Bishop Fraser wrote to Edward warning that at a recent parley between the Scots and English ambassadors at Perth Robert Bruce of Annandale 'who before did not intend to come to the foresaid meeting came with a great following to confer with some who were there'. Bruce had undeniably revived his efforts of 1286 and was canvassing military support to press his claim to the throne with force. He was not without hope of success. According to Fraser:

> 'the earls of Mar and Atholl [earldoms in the north-east of Scotland] are already gathering their army, and

some other nobles of the land join themselves to their party and on that account there is fear of a general war and a great slaughter of men'.

In the face of this calamity the Bishop did not shirk at recommending Edward to 'deal' with John Balliol as the best means of preserving the 'honour and advantage' which the Maid's marriage would have brought and 'for the consolidation of the Scottish people and for saving the shedding of blood'. This was as good as a nomination for the best claimant to the throne from the leader of Scotland's Church.

The forty-year-old John Balliol for his part was clearly aware of this support and chose this moment to make his first decisive personal imprint on the succession crisis: he had, after all, just inherited full possession of his mother's lordship of Galloway. Thus in November 1290 John, styling himself 'heir of the kingdom of Scotland', granted lands in Northumberland to Bishop Bek, Edward's fixer (who may have suggested this act): the other English envoy in Scotland that year was none other than John de Warenne, Earl of Surrey, Balliol's father-in-law. These were surely signs that the English king, too, knew that Balliol had the best legal claim (with Comyn and Scottish ecclesiastical backing to boot) when he summoned a joint Anglo-Scottish parliament to meet on the border at Norham in May 1291.

The Bruces' reply also makes it clear that they were painfully aware of this superior Balliol claim and support. Apparently out-manned militarily by the Comyns, Annandale and Carrick resorted to propaganda and vented their frustrations of the last five years. Their so-called 'Appeal of the Seven Earls' to Edward I was a clumsy attempt to hijack the ancient authority of Scotland's oldest titles (some of which were actually vacant at the time) by claiming that these lords agreed that Bruce the elder was 'the legitimate and true heir-designate'. It then accused the Bishop of St Andrews and John Comyn of Badenoch of colluding to press Balliol's claim 'to our prejudice and the hindrance of our right' as well as of imposing themselves as Guardians, appointing their own officers and of attacking the lands of Mar, Garioch, Moray and others. In the face of this *impasse*, the Appeal called upon Edward to give 'full judgement' over a legal process to decide between the main claimants for the kingship.

6. The ruins of Norham Castle, Northumberland.
It was here, a month before the 'Great Cause' opened in Berwick, that the damage to Scottish independence was really done when Edward I asked the divided Scots to recognise his overlordship.

It cannot, then, have come as a surprise to anyone that, when Edward I upped the stakes at Norham by demanding that each of the thirteen hopeful claimants to the throne recognise him as the feudal lord of the kingdom of Scotland, Robert Bruce of Annandale was the first to do so by 5 June. Edward had first of all asked the Scottish Guardians to submit to his overlordship. But the Bishop of Glasgow's unconvincing reply that they were without 'a head' or king who alone could answer such an unprecedented(!) question really betrayed the Scots' total inability to present a united front: by this stage Edward's intervention was precisely what so many of them sought. John Balliol and the Comyns, however, remained apparently aloof from the so-called 'process of Norham' – despite the presence of English troops – until the eleventh hour: Balliol submitted last to Edward on 11 June only after the leading English claimant, Robert Hastings, and various foreign contenders.

This was the fatal moment and Edward knew it. He had long since ordered his lawyers to search for documentary proof of the English monarchy's claim to Scotland. Not only did Edward now secure the resignation into his hands of all Scottish castles and revenues during the hearings which would follow but he circulated copies of all the submissions, obliged Balliol and the Comyns to repeat their oaths and adjusted the record to show that all the claimants (most of whom held lands of him in England) had acquiesced by 4 June. In early July, Edward cemented these concessions with an extensive ayre around Lowland Scotland taking homages to his overlordship from lesser Scots to add to those already given by the four Guardians, eight earls and fifteen barons – though only one further bishop. He also appointed English officials to collect Scottish funds, authorised the hearing of minor Scottish legal appeals in English courts and attempted to bribe key Scottish nobles with lands.

The Scots' divisions and lack of resolve had thus played right into Edward's hands and continued to do so. Bruce and Balliol (who was aided by Comyn) now had to choose forty auditors each to represent their interests in legal proceedings at Berwick in front of the English king as judge and alongside his own twenty-four jurors. But once seated there was an almost immediate adjournment for ten months. This was to allow Florence, Count of Holland, to substantiate his spurious claim to the throne. What this really did, though, was leave Edward firmly in charge of the Scottish realm for over eighteen months. But the outcome of what is now known as the 'Great Clause' – and which must have been a court-room drama *par excellence* – was surely a foregone conclusion. Bruce the Competitor of Annandale knew as much. His argument that he was nearest by degree to the Canmores as the son of a daughter of Earl David of Huntingdon could not displace Balliol's claim as nearest by blood as a grandson of David's eldest girl. Bruce's last minute attempts, too, to cut deals with Holland and Hastings which would have led to the division of the realm among the leading claimants like a knight's fief were desperate measures. In the end, when Edward announced John Balliol as 'king of Scots' on 7 November 1292 justice had been served: the presence of the majority of earls, prelates, Guardians and crown officers as Balliol auditors did indeed underline John's *de facto* election as 'ruling party candidate'. Balliol and the Comyns now had the legitimate authority with which to hammer the Bruces into submission. However, this had been achieved at the terrible cost of surrendering their autonomy to Longshanks.

3

KING JOHN I OF
SCOTLAND, 1292–96

'We cannot any longer endure these injuries, insults
and grievous wrongs, nor these hostile attacks, nor can
we remain in your fealty and homage (which, it may
be said, were extorted by extreme coercion on your
part) and we desire to assert ourselves against you...'
                    Letter of John I to Edward I, 5 April 1296

The seal of the Guardians (1286–92) had born an image of the
cross of St Andrew and a legend invoking that apostle to 'be the
leader of the compatriot Scots'. The breaking of that seal by the
English king and the commissioning of a new chancery stamp for
King John following his inauguration as king of Scots at Scone on
St Andrews' day 1292 seemed to bode well for Balliol's new royal
regime, a launch pad from which it could continue the work of
Alexander III. However, it is only recently that historians have
sought to rehabilitate John's reputation and achievements as king,
questioning his traditional image as a pathetic, ill-fated monarch at
the beck and call of Edward I.

7. Seal of King John (1292–6)
The Bruce Scots would later insist that John 'was king bot a litill quhile' but
in fact he showed a will to continue the work of Alexander III.

As has often been said, if John Balliol was a puppet king, he was
a puppet of the Comyns whose party clearly ran most of his
everyday government. In this sense, in an age of intense personal
monarchy, John has left little or no stamp of his own character on
his short period of rule. Part of this impression is due to the scant
survival of documents from this period of war, English looting and
later Bruce propaganda. Yet the mere twenty or so extant royal acts
from John's reign paint a picture of a middle-aged king with little
energy or enthusiasm for travelling about his kingdom to assert and
expand the Crown's authority: that was surely left to the Comyns
and their vast affinity.

Nonetheless, annual parliaments appear to have been held under
John. The backlog of legal cases since 1286 was processed and new
sheriffdoms were pencilled in for the west-coast shires of Kintyre,
Argyll and Skye to be policed in turn by James Steward and the
Comyn in-laws, the Macdougalls and the Earl of Ross. King John
also used his family connections to invite merchants from Picardy
to trade with Scotland. Moreover, Balliol's regime has been praised
for its relative ability to stifle the intransigence of the Bruces.

The venerable Bruce of Annandale, now in his seventies, had
resigned his claim to the kingship to his son, the Earl of Carrick,

even before Balliol had been installed as king. The middle Bruce for his part was determined to avoid giving fealty and homage to a new monarch he despised. His attempts to resign his own earldom in turn to his son so as to avoid this obligation of formal submission were blocked in parliament by the Balliol regime until August 1293 when the lobbying of the Earls of Atholl and Mar (Robert Bruce the youngest's new father-in-law) proved decisive. Yet beyond this defiance the Bruces might be said to have been relegated to peripheral and local matters. They did manage to secure Isabella Bruce's marriage to Eric of Norway in 1293 and a Bruce candidate was imposed over a Balliol- and English-favoured man in the vacant bishopric of Galloway (or Whithorn) in 1294. But Robert Bruce the youngest, now twenty, did have to give homage to King John. With two Balliol sons to succeed, Edward and Henry, John's dynasty seemed set fair to deny Robert and his four brothers what their grandfather must have seared into their beings as their birth-right.

But there remained, of course, Edward I's agenda and it was this which fatally compromised Balliol's authority. English officials had ominously overseen John's inauguration at Scone, taking the place of the traditional Scottish magnates, the Earls of Fife and Strathearn. But still not satisfied with Balliol's renewed homage to him as overlord of Scotland on 26 December 1292, a fortnight later Edward had obliged John to free him from any promises he may have made during the period 1290–92. In one moment, all the protection sought by the Scottish bishops and barons in the treaty of Birgham and pre-conditions for the release of the kingdom after the Great Cause were swept away. The English king set about exploiting his jurisdiction ruthlessly. Not only would he bill Balliol for over £4,500 inheritance tax and the administration fees of his installation: but also before John had settled on his throne English courts were hearing Scottish legal appeals.

Many of these cases were brought by Scots and foreign plaintiffs who were clearly aggrieved by Balliol's elevation as king and by the Comyns' territorial and political grip on much of the kingdom. There was litigation by the Count of Holland and Eric of Norway (trying to recover the Maid's dowry), as well as English clerics challenging the Bishop of St Andrews, a MacDonald complaint against the Macdougalls and the most awkward case brought by the

8. John's submission to Edward I, 1292–3.
After he renewed his homage to Edward I as overlord of Scotland in December 1292, John was required a month later to free the English king from any guarantees he had made about Scottish government.

MacDuffs of Fife. Significantly, many of these appeals may have been encouraged by Bruce of Annandale (until his death in 1295) and his title-less son (who now became keeper of Carlisle in north-west England for Edward). But it was the English king himself who was most keen to stoke such harrying of Balliol's independence, paying the costs of many of these litigants to journey to London.

But when Edward summoned the new Scottish king south as his vassal to answer these legal claims in person it must be remembered that John and his advisors did attempt to resist. As well as refusing to attend English parliaments at York or Westminster, John also insisted he could not answer any charges without first 'consulting the trusted men of his realm' in council· his bishops and noble councillors also dispatched letters of protest. But ultimately, Balliol – for most of his adult life a tenant of Edward I – was only capable of 'firmness and pliancy'. When threatened with the seizure of Scottish royal castles on the border Balliol crumbled, came south, renewed his homage to the English Crown and gave ground in these cases.

In the end it would require a far more general threat to the livelihood of all significant subjects for the Scots to openly defy Edward I. As ever in Scottish history this situation was precipitated by developments outwith that small kingdom, driven by the intensive rivalry between England and France. By spring 1294 Edward had, ironically, refused to maintain his own homage to Philip IV of France for the duchy of Acquitaine in Gascony and the thunder of war beckoned. As was his perceived feudal right Edward summoned his key subjects to do military service: this included John and at least ten Scottish earls and lords with their armed followings. Fighting in a strange land at their own cost had been one of the Scots' fears expressed in the Birgham treaty. Now it was made real. The last time a Scottish king and his subjects had fought for an English monarch in France or Flanders – under Malcolm IV in 1160 – there had been a rebellion in Scotland upon their return, lashing out at the unwelcome closeness of their king with his southern neighbour. This time the Scottish leaders refused to let things progress so far.

According to English chroniclers, at this point King John was removed from full power and a council of twelve Scottish churchmen and nobles assumed responsibility for approaching the French to secure an alliance (which would also include Norway). In reality, Balliol's French lands and connections must have aided the Scottish envoys. Indeed, one of the terms of support concluded by October 1295 stipulated that John's heir, Edward Balliol, would wed a niece of Philip IV. However, the Scottish embassy of John Soules, Ingelram d'Umphraville and the Bishops of St Andrews and Dunkeld, may otherwise have found terms dictated to them by the French. The rest of what is now hailed as the first treaty of 'auld alliance' between Scotland and France against the 'auld enemie', England, was certainly one-sided: if the French were invaded by Edward, the Scots would attack him but if the Scots were invaded by the English, the French gave only a vague promise to help and advise in what ways they could. The Scots may have been encouraged to take what they could get by Edward's apparent problems at home – a Welsh revolt from late 1294 to March 1295 – and his greater interest in French conquest. But, after a year of quashing one set of rebellious vassals, when Edward heard about the treaty he was furious: he postponed his French campaign and turned to the north.

For Edward in early 1296, the campaign to Scotland was always a domestic police action but it was one nonetheless conducted at the outset by employing the full force of England's experienced bureaucracy of war. Some 30,000 men were called to host at Wark in March that year, including several divisions of cavalry and crossbow/longbow archers selected by county 'commissioners of array'. Well blooded in French and Welsh wars, their numbers were also swollen by well-paid mercenaries and many European knights keen to earn their spurs in the service of the formidable fifty-seven-year-old English warrior king. All would be paid and supplied throughout the war by English shipping along the east coast.

The Scots by comparison were much less militarised. The Comyns and others could field a substantial host as John's generals. But at best this amounted to 20,000 men doing their duty of 'Scottish' service for up to forty days a year without pay or supplies with an elite core of perhaps only a few hundred mounted knights, esquires and men-at-arms. The vast majority of Scotland's troops brandished only poorly maintained spears and axes on foot. More significantly, the Scots and their leaders were little experienced in war in hot blood. Even the Comyns had last fought in anger in the doomed English royal army at Lewes in 1264 or on crusade in 1270–2: only 1,000 or so had fought for James the Steward against the Norse at Largs as long ago as 1263. Nor should it be assumed that the extra adrenaline and courage of fighting to protect their homeland would always give the Scots extra steel. In what was really still a matter of high politics, many ordinary tenants and some quite significant Scottish landlords with lands in England might not have been prepared to die in a jurisdictional argument about overlordship: at the end of the day it mattered little who was feudal superior and the concept of nation and patriotism – of being either Scottish or English – was in no way fully formed.

Worse still, King John, the Comyns and their close supporters must have feared the danger to be had from within their borders from disappointed nobles who preferred to side with the English king.

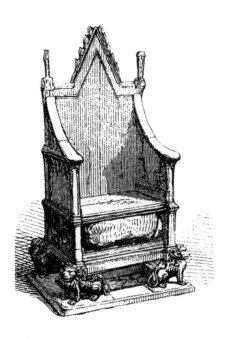

9. The Stone of Scone under the Westminster coronation chair.
Last used to inaugurate John I in 1292, removed as a war trophy by Edward I in 1296,
withheld from the Bruce Scots as part of the peace of 1328 and only returned finally to
Scotland in 1996.

10. Toom Tabard, 1296.
After his surrender at Brechin in July 1296 Balliol was stripped of his regalia and taken
south as a prisoner: this is the image of the king which has persisted to this day.

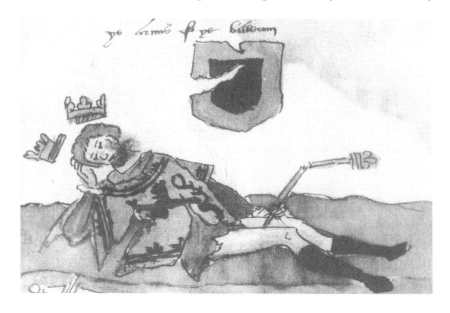

This of course included the Bruces who did homage to Edward I on 25 March 1296 and joined his army: but it also included other magnates like the Earls of Angus and March and, perhaps, the MacDonalds and Earls of Ross and Strathearn. King John's forfeiture of Carrick and Annandale in reply was a measure which might easily be reversed as the English king did the Bruces' hard work for them in overawing the Balliol regime.

And Edward's victory was seemingly swift and total. On 30 March his army made a swift example of the townspeople of Scotland's leading sea-port, Berwick-upon-Tweed, slaughtering up to 7,000 inhabitants. The Scots host, meanwhile – led by John Comyn, Earl of Buchan – had adopted what would become a traditional Scottish tactic, dodging the invader and attacking northern England. However, in descending upon Carlisle and its hinterland about 27–9 March, this really ineffectual assault also targeted the interests of the regime's domestic antagonists, the Bruces, as the elder Bruce was keeper of this English market-town and castle garrison and the Scots marched through Annandale *en route*. Yet this pre-emptive strike before Balliol had even renounced his homage only angered Edward I and left the kingdom's east flank exposed. When a small Scottish force attempted to relieve the besieged castle of Dunbar – held by the Earl of March's wife, a Comyn – both Buchan and King John were absent. In the ensuing battle at Dunbar of 27 April the Scots were defeated resoundingly by a small English force led by Surrey, Balliol's father-in-law.

Edward then progressed north unhindered – beyond the Forth, through St Andrews and into Tayside. As the English drove straight for the heart of Comyn power in the north-east, the Scots' leaders soon lost all stomach for the fight. At Kincardine, about 2 July, King John surrendered himself along with the Comyns. A week later in Strathcaro churchyard near Brechin Edward personally oversaw the stripping of John's vestments of office, seizing and breaking his standard, coronet, sceptre and orb, leaving him forever in the eyes of history as 'Toom Tabard' – empty surcoat. Shortly thereafter, while the Comyns, Murrays, bishops and other Scottish notables entered prison, King John and his sons were transported to the Tower of London along with the stone of Scone and the Scottish Crown's valuables, relics and records. Only John would never return.

4

THE SCOTTISH REBELLION, 1296–1302

'Have we nothing to do but win kingdoms for you?'
Edward I to Robert Bruce the elder, 1296.

As Scottish castles fell and Balliol's lieges surrendered, the Bruces must have felt that the just reward for their loyalty to Edward I should be the vassal kingship of Scotland. Yet the English king's impatient reply, quoted above, made it clear that Scotland was no longer to be treated as a kingdom but merely as a conquered land, an English province. Although there was no wholesale forfeiture of Scottish landowners, after sufficient homages to Edward had been collected from Lowland Scots and their names recorded on a 'Ragman's Roll' an English colonial administration was installed. This was to be headed by Surrey as Lieutenant, the odious Hugh Cressingham as treasurer and a raft of English garrison commanders as sheriffs. The untrustworthy and self-serving Bruces were even to be denied local office by Edward.

However, now for the first time, the majority of ordinary Scots – from Berwick to Urquhart – encountered the invader. The presence of an occupation regime while many of the realm's natural leaders were incarcerated brought with it restrictions on people's movements and vital economic activity as well as rude interruptions to custom and the imposition of a rigorous taxation system: Cressingham, indeed, would collect over £5,000 from the Scots in his first year of office. The English garrisons, too, often speaking with a foreign accent or tongue, were surely responsible for some individual acts of atrocity although they also brought economic opportunity to some areas.

All of this meant that even before Edward I left Scotland for Gascony in August 1296 there were rumblings of rebellion in various corners of the realm. But the available evidence suggests that the full-scale risings which had erupted in particular localities by the spring of 1297 were still incited and often co-ordinated into a concerted campaign by the realm's natural leaders, the nobility and prelates. Predictably, rebellion took hold in those areas where the English occupation was at its thinnest and soon exposed Edward's over-confident assumption of control after his push-over victory. The first Scottish leader to really emerge was Andrew Murray, son of the Lord of Bothwell in Lanarkshire and Avoch in Moray. He led the north-eastern tenants of his captive father to join up with Macdougall men in the Great Glen to over-run the garrisons of Urquhart and Inverlochy as well as to attack the lands of local rivals (and Edward's allies), the MacDonalds and Earl of Ross. When the English king released the Comyns from temporary service in France to return to Scotland to hunt Murray down, these lords stalled for time and allowed Murray to levy their followers of Buchan and Badenoch and to live off their lands: these lords reported to the English the escape of the rebel army into 'bog and wood'.

Murray's success caused doubts about the English regime to spread. The Macduffs rebelled in Fife only to be captured by the man they attacked, Malise, Earl of Strathearn: it is, though, telling of the uncertain state of play that Malise declined to hand them over to the English. But, of course, it was the armed rising of William Wallace in the west and south-west which has had most impact on historical memory. This strapping, charismatic, 'bloody man... a leader of brigands' was probably already an outlaw from the occupation regime before, as the English chroniclers assert, he

11. William Wallace.
This inspiring Scottish leader, fighting above all to restore an independent
Scottish kingdom, may have considered changing sides from Balliol to
Bruce about 1299.

was directed by his local superiors, Bishop Wishart of Glasgow and James the Steward, to lead a wider rebellion. Beginning with the destruction of the garrison of Ayr and attacks on an English justiciar at Scone and a siege of Dundee (where he was joined by Sir William Douglas), Wallace's support quickly mushroomed out from the Stewart lands in the west.

By early summer the various resistance cells were clearly in contact with each other. On 4 June 1297 Cressingham reported to Edward that:

> 'there are many persons who disturb the peace and quietness of our kingdom [Scotland] and make diverse meetings, conventicles and conspiracies in very many parts of the land... and perpetrate depredations, burnings, robberies, rapines and other evils'.

He also revealed his fears about the fragmentary state of the English regime reporting that:

> 'by far the greater part of your counties of the realm of Scotland are still unprovided with keepers... some have given up their bailliewicks and others dare not return; and in some counties the Scots have established and placed bailiffs and ministers so that no county is in its proper order excepting Berwick and Roxburgh'.

It was this ill-motivated, under-paid and under-supplied administration which Edward looked to to crush the rising with force.

But before a telling confrontation could take place, the awkward question of in just whose name the rebellion was to be fought was posed. With the Balliol dynasty locked up in London, the youngest Robert Bruce, Earl of Carrick, now aged twenty-three, saw a ripe opportunity to seize the initiative in directing the community's war-effort and advancing his own kin's cause for the throne. Colluding with the Steward and Wishart – who would later insist that they had supported the Bruce claim to the throne throughout 1286–92 – Bruce rose up in arms in the south-west. According to a contemporary English chronicler, Bruce may have been genuinely torn between feelings of loyalty to his father (who remained in Carlisle) and his own growing sense of patriotism as a Carrick-born man drawn to 'join my nation from which I am born'. Yet ultimately ambition, lands and self-preservation came first. Bruce failed to inspire the tenantry of Annandale and his rising was quickly aborted: he and his confederates capitulated to the English once more at Irvine in Ayrshire in June 1297.

Wallace was sufficiently disgusted by this attempt to hijack the revolution as to attack the Bishop of Glasgow's property. His behaviour as Guardian in 1298, too, suggests that William was at first committed to fight for the cause of the rightful king, John, as was Andrew Murray. These two generals now joined forces in late summer 1297. Their famous destruction of Cressingham and Surrey's army at the battle of Stirling Bridge on 11 September was thus as much a body-blow to the Bruce cause as to the English conquest.

However, with the advantage of hindsight, it might be argued that the great mistake of the nobility of the Balliol-Comyn party was in not coming out in full active support of Wallace after this triumph. In truth, most Scots surely saw the writing on the wall: that an enraged Edward I would now spare no expense in crushing Scottish rebels. Better then for the Scots' natural leaders to hide behind the figures of Wallace and (until his death from wounds in late 1297) Murray as commanders of 'the army of the kingdom of Scotland' rather than to risk openly their lives and lands. Many men, besides, cannot have been convinced that the cause was worth reviving out of personal loyalty to the timid and imprisoned King John. Nonetheless, Wallace's attempts to attract foreign traders back to Scotland, his raiding of northern England in the winter of 1297–8 and his assumption of the post of Guardian by March 1298 were all moves made in that sovereign's name. That John was at least the legitimate figurehead through whom the Scots could revive their independent kingdom was underlined by Scottish ecclesiastical embassies to the Pope in Rome and to the king of France from 1298 onwards. These were efforts Wallace himself boosted by appointing the Glasgow man, William Lamberton, as the new Bishop of St Andrews. A bit more united effort by the community behind these stratagems might have brought early success for Balliol.

That said, Wallace did not have to risk everything in battle against the English king. More gain might have been had in stringing along Edward's huge army of 24,000 men as it entered Scotland in summer 1298, depriving them of supplies and then declining to fight. But when Wallace did engage the 16,000 English, Welsh and Irish troops that remained on 22 July his host may have been sorely compromised by the irresolution of the Scottish nobility. The tradition that it was the Comyns who betrayed Wallace at the battle of Falkirk by withdrawing their cavalry may be later Bruce propaganda. But Robert Bruce, Earl of Carrick, may himself have opted to side with the English at that time. On the day, Edward I's superior archery and horse-power overwhelmed Wallace's three divisions of spearmen in schiltrons (or hedgehogs): noble fence-sitting was thus proven to be wise.

Defeated, Wallace resigned the Guardianship. But if Edward's complete re-conquest of Scotland had been expected it never materialised. Although the defeat at Stirling had actually allowed the English king to rally support from his disgruntled subjects, a lack of money, motivation and the preference for the glory and lands to be won in France prevented an effective English regime from once more attempting to police the difficult terrain, climate and people of Scotland after victory at Falkirk. Into the resulting power-vacuum stepped the younger generation of Scottish nobles as it dawned on them that Longshanks was in no position to enforce his will.

By late 1298, indeed, John Comyn, son of the Lord of Badenoch and nephew of King John, had emerged as co-guardian with the unlikely Robert Bruce, Earl of Carrick. As in 1286, 1289 and 1297 what the Bruces surely hoped to achieve was not the success of the Balliol claim but to turn the community to serve their own dynastic ends. The captivity of John and his sons must have been a potent argument to persuade key Scots to abandon the Balliols as a lost cause and to revive the kingship under a Bruce. This factional agenda formed the backdrop to a much more low-key Scottish military campaign for the next two years. Confining themselves to raiding and avoiding sieges and pitched battles, the Scottish captains, spread throughout central and south-western Scotland, aimed to keep the Edwardian regime confined to the border shires and castles while Scottish clerics pressed on with the alternative tack of diplomatic overtures to the Pope.

It was in this uncertain, tense wartime situation that the rival guardians' suspicions got the better of them. According to an English spy, the Scottish war council held at Peebles on 19 August 1299 erupted into a fist-fight with the Comyns accusing Bruce, William and Malcolm Wallace and the Bishop of St Andrews of 'lèse majesté' or treason. What they understandably feared was that Bruce had persuaded those men most active in attempting to restore the kingdom that Balliol should be dropped and the willing and present alternative of Bruce himself be backed as king.

Yet it is likely that this bust-up took place before the Scots had had firm word that their embassies to Paris and Rome had produced some results in Balliol's favour. On 28 June 1299, Pope Boniface VIII – so persuaded by Scottish churchmen's pleas that Edward I had attacked Scotland, a 'special daughter' of Rome, when that realm had been without a head – ordered the English king to provide written proof within six months of his claims as overlord. In the end, Edward would not receive this papal bull until August 1300 and only reply in 1301. But long before then simultaneous pressure from the Pope and his sometime controller, Philip IV of France (against whom England's war was not going well), had obliged Edward to make a significant concession. On 18 July 1299 he ordered the release of John Balliol into papal custody at Avignon in Provençe. As this was done in advance of an Anglo-French truce and plans for the widower Edward himself to wed Philip IV's sister and for his son to wed Philip's daughter in September 1299, the English king must have hoped Balliol's transfer would ease his diplomatic position.

Bishop Lamberton may thus have returned to Scotland in summer 1299 with news of the papal bull ('Scimus Filii') but not King John's parole: the Comyns and their allies might easily have suspected the prelate and his patron, Wallace, of transferring their allegiances to the candidate at liberty, Bruce: this may also explain why William Wallace seems to have been detained by the king of France for a spell in 1299–1300 before being allowed to pass on to Rome. The Comyns' fear of being displaced as the community's leaders also seems to have caused them to lash out at their local rivals: for it was also revealed at the 1299 council that an 'Alexander Comyn and Lachlan were burning and devastating the district they were in [the north-west], attacking the people of Scotland'. It may therefore have been to avoid full-blown civil war that the council – calmed by James Steward and others – used Bishop Lamberton's mandate of the papal bull (and, if word arrived, Balliol's release) to appoint him 'principal captain': he was now Chief-Guardian with control of royal castles above Comyn and Bruce. At the very least, though, the Scots may have kept their options open by allowing Bruce to remain: after all, Edward Balliol remained a captive in England.

But a little under a year later Robert Bruce was gone. The report of another English agent in May 1300 asserts that at a parliament at Rutherglen near Glasgow, Bishop Lamberton and Comyn were again openly at odds. This time the Steward and David Strathbogie, Earl of Atholl, 'held to the party of the bishop': these three would all come out for Bruce as king in 1306. Thus this conflict may again have been rooted in suspicions that a section of the community were working for the absent Earl of Carrick. However, as we shall see, diplomatic talks which would favour Balliol's cause were then well advanced and the arguments amongst the Scottish political community may simply have been over lands, offices and authority. Certainly, matters were eased by replacing Carrick as guardian with Ingelram d'Umphraville, brother of the Earl of Angus, a solid Balliol-Comyn man and one of the ambassadors to Paris in 1295: it was also decided that another parliament would be called once the Comyn Earl of Buchan had returned from raising troops in the Balliol lordship of Galloway.

Thus by 1300 the younger Bruce was frozen out by both the English and Scottish regimes. As the fighting concentrated itself in south-west Scotland around key castles like Caerlaverock and the Bruce seat in Annandale at Lochmaben this put him in an extremely difficult position. Robert can only have watched on from the sidelines as the Scots survived three Edwardian invasions throughout 1300–02, each campaign in turn escalating in scale with separate armies dispatched to march through the south-west towards Ayrshire and Glasgow under Edward, Prince of Wales, and the Earl of Ulster while Edward I himself devastated the east march towards Edinburgh, Stirling and Perth. An English victory and Scottish collapse might have done more to aid Bruce's cause at this juncture. But annual English problems with logistics and in finding money and men for near-mutinous garrisons made this an impossibility.

So too did the Scots' success in ensuring that Philip IV insisted that Scotland be included in several Anglo-French truces in this period as an ally of France. Bruce was also unable to influence the Scots' ongoing campaign of words in Paris and Rome (although he was kept closely informed of both). It was here that the Balliol cause seemed to have an increasing chance of a breakthrough. On 7 May 1301 Edward I finally replied to Boniface VIII's demand that he show proof of his overlordship of Scotland. This missive, delivered by clerical lawyers, cited amongst its many arguments the willing Scottish submissions to England in 1174 and 1291 and the historical claim (based on Geoffrey of Monmouth's *History of the Kings of Britain* of *c.*1136) that the three kingdoms of the British Isles had been gifted in antiquity by Brutus the Trojan to his three sons with the elder claiming England and thus having a right to be overlord of the other two, Scotland and Wales.

The reply of the Scottish churchmen from St Andrews already present in Rome was arguably a much more considered, lawyerly and persuasive retort. True, the Scots also recited their own national creation myth: this consisted of the journey of 'Gathelos', a Greek Prince, and 'Scota', daughter of a Pharoah, exiles from two ancient cultures (one victorious over the Trojans) who led their people via Spain and Ireland to establish Scotland (from 'Scota') about the time of Moses. But the Scots also offered solid documentary proofs in the form of the English annulment of overlordship over William I for Scotland from 1189, the homages of Alexanders II and III only for lands in England and the 'special daughter' status of Scotland under Rome.

The Scottish lobby probably carried the day at the *curia*. However, the cold fact remains that John Balliol's further release (confirmed on 1 October 1301) from papal control into Philip IV's hands had far more to do with the French need for a diplomatic lever against Edward I. Nonetheless, this second transfer – presumably involving a move for Balliol to his family lands in Picardy – further energised the Scots. As early as May 1301 John Soules, another of the Paris ambassadors of 1295, had been named sole Guardian for Scotland issuing acts in King John's name. Soules and the prelates thus left the fighting up to the Comyns, Umphraville, David Barclay of Brechin, James Steward, the Mowbrays, Macdowells and Macdougalls and others in the south-west while further efforts were made to secure Balliol's final return to Scotland, ideally with the backing of a French expeditionary force.

By early 1302 all parties concerned shared a strong sense that a Balliol restoration was a distinct possibility. A nine-month truce declared in France on 26 January 1302 was also to include the Scots. Under its terms Edward I promised to hand over to Balliol's keepers, the French, temporary control of the Scottish territory he had recovered from the Guardians in 1301. That this land included much of Carrick must have given the younger Robert Bruce considerable pause for thought. But when a great Scottish embassy – including Soules, Comyn of Buchan, Umphraville, a William Balliol, James Steward and the Bishops of St Andrews and Dunkeld – set out for Paris in February 1302 Bruce could afford to wait no longer. On 16 February 1302, perhaps through the offices of his father, keeper of Carlisle, Robert came out of the cold and once more gave his homage to Edward I.

This time, however, he managed to extract the English king's written promise that not only would he guarantee Bruce's claim to his family lands in Scotland as well as those of Mar (his father-in-law) and Umphraville (his replacement as guardian in 1300); but Edward also promised that:

> 'because he [Bruce] fears that the kingdom of Scotland may be removed from out of the king's hands (which God forbid!) and handed over to Sir John Balliol or to his son, or that the right be brought into dispute, or reversed and contradicted in a fresh judgement, the king grants to Robert that he may pursue his right and the king will hear him fairly and hold him to justice in the king's court...[or] elsewhere than in the king's court'.

ANO EFTER KING ROBERT
YE BRVCE MARIIT YE
DVKE OF HVLLESTERIS DOCHTER

12. Robert Bruce, Earl of Carrick, and his second wife, Elizabeth de Burgh.
Bruce's submission to the English in 1302, out of fear for a Balliol return to Scotland, at
least brought him a new wife in the daughter of the Earl of Ulster.

This was clearly a pact which at least on paper guaranteed Bruce's right to claim the kingship should there be a need to re-open the Great Cause, either in England or under papal jurisdiction. At this juncture, this was the only means by which Robert might secure the Scottish throne.

5

SECRECY AND MURDER, 1302-06

'John Balliol... of his own accord... uttered a statement... to this effect: namely, that when he possessed and ruled the realm of Scotland as king and lord of the realm, he found in the men of that realm such malice, deceit, treason and treachery, arising from their malignity, wickedness and stratagems, and from various other execrable and detestable actions by those who, as he had good grounds to believe were plotting to poison him, who was then their prince, that it is not his intention to enter or go into the realm of Scotland at any time to come...'

Recorded by notary, London, 21 April 1298

A little over a year before he had been obliged to release John Balliol into papal custody in 1299, Edward I had extracted this propaganda statement from his captive. In some senses it may reflect a quite genuine apathy on John's part about his lost kingdom. But in early 1302 the Balliol cause seemed to be in the ascendant and the Scottish envoys to Paris were prepared to put all their eggs in the French basket.

However, all too typically, the needs of the two greater kingdoms overtook events in the smaller. On 11 July 1302 an army of French cavalry was devastated by the spearmen of the Flemish town of Courtrai in a victory far more revolutionary in its military implications than Wallace's triumph at Stirling. The French now desperately needed peace and on 2 December 1302 they secured the treaty of Amiens: this time the Scots were not included. Thus not only was Edward I free to concentrate all his resources on re-conquering Scotland but the Scots were denied their king and the services of their many ambassador generals who were kept in France: the Pope also had no time for the Scots. In January 1303 the Bishop of St Andrews could only write stoically to William Wallace – who must have been privy to the Scots diplomacy in his travels to Paris and Rome in 1299–1301 – reassuring him of material support and urging him to help the Scots take heart in John Comyn of Badenoch's recent victory in a skirmish at Roslin: Lamberton clearly knew the survival of the Scottish war effort must now depend once more upon such men of independent character as Sir William.

This attempt to rouse the troops was not without effect. It would take Edward I over eighteen months to re-conquer Scotland in a three-pronged campaign. Unlike in 1296, he now faced dogged resistance from Scots who refused to fight pitched battles of chivalry. Moreover, Scottish captains like Comyn, Wallace and Sir Simon Fraser may have been further provoked by fears of attacks upon their own lands and goods by Scots in English pay: this included Robert Bruce of Carrick who served in the English host alongside his new father-in-law, the Earl of Ulster.

Nonetheless, by early 1304 it was all but over and on 9 February John Comyn sought terms for his surrender. That Longshanks was determined to have his revenge and make an example to the Scottish community is made clear first of all by his cruel insistence on refusing to take the surrender of Stirling Castle garrison until June 1304, bombarding its walls and occupants holding 'of the Lion' with stone shot from his new trebuchet, the 'Warwolf'; and, secondly, by his demand that certain Scots would only be forgiven when they brought in William Wallace who was to be denied a pardon. However, the fact that the English king was prepared to talk terms with Comyn and others underlines the fact that he had learnt an important lesson from his failed attempt to exclude the Scots from the governance of their realm in 1296. Without the Scottish establishment's acquiescence the northern kingdom would be too expensive and hostile to hold. So in 1304 this meant securing an understanding with the Comyns and their allies in the Guardianship: it also meant Edward would have to break his word with the untrustworthy outsider, Bruce.

Thus while Edward promised Comyn that the laws, customs and institutions of Scotland would be upheld and that he and his confederates trapped in Paris could retain their lands and offices after short periods of exile, Bruce began to look to his own interests once more. In doing so, Robert may have been acting upon a welcome sense of release after the death of his father in April 1304. Now the eldest Bruce heir to the throne, Carrick seems to have been more readily prepared to sacrifice his family's English lands for what he perceived as his true Scottish destiny. But he proceeded with stealth. As Edward and his royal household applauded the spectacle of Stirling Castle's punishment (a siege to which Bruce evaded sending siege engines of his own), the Earl of Carrick met with Bishop Lamberton at nearby Cambuskenneth Abbey: here they concluded a secret pact to support each other in the 'urgent enterprises' ahead. In doing so, Bruce secured the blessing of a leading champion of the Scottish community and cause, just as Balliol had done through Bishop Fraser in 1290: for Lamberton there remained no other viable option if he was to protect his national Church.

Throughout the remainder of 1304 and into 1305 Robert would have gone on logically to sound out the support of many other nobles and prelates – especially in the south-west – for a Bruce bid for the kingship. However, there remained the difficulty of disentangling these men from commitment to Edward I's plans for Scotland's future governance. To this, at first, Bruce seems to have had considerable input. He was not only made sheriff of Lanark and Ayr but along with Bishop Wishart of Glasgow (an English captive since 1297) Bruce was the sole Scottish representative at a parliament at Westminster in March 1305 which made preliminary preparations to draw up an Ordinance of rule for the land of Scotland. But the Scottish assembly at Scone in May 1305 which this English parliament asked to nominate ten delegates to attend a further meeting in England to finalise the details of this administration was clearly a Comyn-dominated forum. Bruce was once again frozen out. The embassy sent south in late summer 1305 included not only the Bishop of St Andrews but also the Bishop of Dunkeld, the Earl of Buchan, John Mowbray, Robert Keith, Adam Gordon and, significantly, John Menteith of Arran and Knapdale, the man who had just betrayed William Wallace. The grisly sight of Wallace's hanging, disembowelling, beheading and quartering at Smithfield in London can only have sharpened the minds of the Scottish delegates to conform with Edward's wishes in drawing up his Ordinance for Scotland's new regime.

On paper at least this settlement was far more statesmanlike than the occupation of 1296. An English Lieutenant would still preside but he would be advised by a Scottish council and chamberlain. Scots were to fill most of the sheriffdoms and four pairs of English and Scottish justiciars were to oversee the higher courts. In addition, Scottish nobles were allowed to pay fines instead of enduring exile and to recover lost lands through the courts. But that the Comyns would continue to lead the community was underlined by the fact that Bruce had now lost even his sheriffdoms.

It was perhaps to discuss the status quo of regional and administrative power in Scotland that Bruce arranged to meet John Comyn of Badenoch on neutral holy ground (half-way between their respective territories in the south-west) on 10 February 1306 in the Greyfriar's Church at Dumfries, while a justiciar court was held in the nearby royal castle. However, it is far more likely that Bruce's canvassing for support for his claim to the kingship had reached the point where he had to be sure either of Comyn's neutrality or his vested interest. According to English chronicle sources, Bruce falsely accused Comyn of betrayal and executed a premeditated plan when he 'struck him with his sword' leaving his brother-in-law, Sir Christopher Seton, along with James Lindsay and Roger Kirkpatrick, to dispatch Comyn and his entourage before the high altar. By contrast, in Scottish chronicle accounts, Comyn was 'the evil speaker' who could not be reasoned with and deserved to die in hot blood. In John Barbour's famous fictional version of these events, *The Bruce*, written in the 1370s, both tales were combined to suggest that sometime *c.*1304–5, near Stirling, Comyn had offered to support a Bruce bid for the throne but then betrayed their indenture to King Edward: Robert had thus killed him in revenge.

In the long-run, the destruction of Comyn of Badenoch gravely weakened the Comyn-Balliol party in Scotland. But in the immediate short-term his sacrilegious slaughter cannot have been pre-arranged. The old personal animosities and frustrations of 1299 between these two ambitious lords must have simply come pouring out. At best, Robert could be said to have been forced by his

13. The murder of John Comyn of Badenoch, February 1306, Dumfries.
The first blow in the civil war which launched Bruce's bid for the kingship
was surely unplanned, born of Robert's frustration with his
Scottish opponents.

precipitate actions to have to put into premature motion already well-laid plans. For now the only protection open to him from both his Scottish enemies and Edward I lay in assuming the office of king. It has been suggested by some historians that Robert did so only after being denied the pardon and protection of Edward I. But the rapid course of events over the next two months suggests that Robert immediately set his sights on Scone.

After seizing Balliol and Comyn castles in the south-west at Dalswinton, Tibbers and Dumfries and mobilising the armed tenantry of Annandale and Carrick, Robert and his small party proceeded to victual the castles of Loch Doon in Carrick and Dunaverty in Kintyre, surely preparing a back door if they needed to flee. But after passing to Glasgow where Bishop Wishart absolved Bruce of his bloody crime and provided him with vestments for a royal inauguration, the new rebels pushed on to Scone by 25 March. Here the attendance was less than regal. Although Bishop Lamberton had managed to slip out of English custody to oversee the improvised ceremony of investiture only a handful of nobles were present: the Earls of Atholl, Menteith, Lennox and Mar, James Steward (who had found it difficult to recover his lands from Edward's placemen), Sir James Douglas (whose father, William, had died in the Tower of London in 1299) as well as Carrick's four brothers, Sir Christopher Seton, Robert Boyd of Noddsdale and other south-western men. Bruce's sisters and his second wife, Elizabeth de Burgh, and his daughter from his first marriage, Marjorie, also participated. Yet so desperate was the usurper regime for further legitimisation that instead of the traditional role in installing any new king upon the stone of Scone to be played by the Earl of Fife – then still a minor in English custody – Robert settled for the blessing of Isabella, Countess of Buchan, the absent Fife Earl's aunt.

No wonder then that Robert's new queen is said to have chided him for 'playing' at king. Yet this was deadly serious. Bruce had now passed the point of no return: he would have to fight a civil and a national war with the same sword.

PART TWO

THE BRUCE CAUSE

1

THE BRUCES' SCOTTISH WAR,
1306–10

'His mishaps, flights and dangers; hardships and
weariness, hunger and thirst; watchings and fastings;
nakedness and cold; snares and banishments; the
seizing, imprisoning, slaughter, and downfall of his
near ones, and – even more – dear ones. No-one now
living, I think, recollects all this.'

Chronicle of John of Fordun, c.1380

Over the next decade and more, Robert I did indeed suffer such
pains and sacrifices in the pursuit of his ultimate goal. Most
students of history are well aware that it is an eternal testament to
Bruce's genius for guerrilla warfare, his choice of able captains and
his sheer guts in leading his men from the front that he was able to
return from the brink of disaster after 1306 to establish his dynasty.
But it is often overlooked that in doing so the Bruce party either
destroyed or forced to submit magnates who before 1304 had been
the mainstay of the Scottish patriotic movement, fighting in arms
and diplomacy to restore their rightful Balliol king and an

independent Scottish realm. This was a Bruce coup. The destruction inflicted upon the land and persons of those who stood in Robert's way often bordered on the same level of vendetta which Edward I had saved for Wallace (and it is certainly interesting to speculate which side that warrior would have chosen had he lived beyond 1305). In many ways this civil war would leave deeper, angrier scars in the Scottish political landscape than the conflict with Plantagenet England.

In his defense, King Robert certainly paid his dues. With news of Comyn's murder, Edward flew into a rage ordering the execution of anyone caught aiding Bruce. He also invited requests from English nobles and churchmen for the lands and offices of Bruce and his supporters in Scotland: now he could motivate his subjects to fight for something in the northern realm. It was an English force under Lieutenant Aymer de Valence which inflicted the first defeat upon Bruce's band as it pushed north towards Comyn territory taking homages with duress, for example, seizing the Earl of Strathearn and forcing him to submit. At Methven near Perth on 19 June Robert's contingent of 1,000 men or so were ambushed losing most of their infantry. Taking the decision to send the womenfolk on to Kildrummy Castle in Mar, Bruce and his closest supporters retreated west on horseback only to be put to flight by Comyn of Badenoch's in-laws, the Macdougalls, at Dail Righ in early July. At the same time, Robert's womenfolk, brother Neil, Christopher Seton and the Earl of Atholl were captured near Tain by the Earl of Ross. Unlike the Steward, James Douglas and the Bishops of St Andrews and Glasgow – who had quickly decided to submit – these Bruce familiars felt the full weight of Edward's wrath: Neil, Seton and Atholl were executed and the ladies gaoled in towers with Countess Isabella of Buchan and Robert's sister, Mary, most notoriously suspended in iron cages.

King Robert was now running for his life and he chose wisely to seek shelter in the Gaelic Irish Sea world he had known as a boy. Probably relying on the support of many of the Isles kindreds who had witnessed the Turnberry band of 1286, the rump of the Bruce faction wintered in and around the Hebrides and Rathlin Island off Ulster (perhaps also sending for aid from their aunt as queen of Norway). This was a lair from which Robert was at least able to draw the refits of Carrick in late 1306. It was with this vital support in the form of supplies, men and ships from the MacDonalds of Islay, MacRuaridhs of Garmoran and Campbells of Lochawe that the Bruces returned to the south-west mainland via Kintyre and Arran in early 1307. Robert, who had lost everything, had no choice but to attempt a come-back.

At first his luck did not improve. An advance landing under Thomas and Alexander Bruce (who may have solicited aid for Robert from the Gaels of Ireland) was betrayed and the brothers captured by the Balliol tenants of Galloway, the Macdowells: Edward had them executed. But under Robert's personal leadership the tide began to turn. Targeting the Balliol lands anew in Galloway, Bruce got the better of skirmishes with English troops at Glen Trool in Galloway in late April and then at Loudoun Hill in Ayrshire on 10 May. The 'royal' army grew in size the longer it survived: as one English chronicler put it – 'despite the fearful vengeance inflicted upon the Scots who adhered to Bruce, the number of those willing to strengthen him in his kingship increased daily'. Bruce had probably already taken the decision to march north to smash the Comyn heartlands before the most welcome (and, in truth, long anticipated) news broke: Edward I had died at Burgh-on-Sands in Cumberland leading his host north to crush the rebels.

This was a real watershed. Despite a testing apprenticeship in the English campaigns in Scotland of 1299–1304, Prince Edward of Caernarvon, now Edward II, would show neither any real inclination or the necessary leadership skills to recover and re-conquer the realm that would once have been his by marriage. A man of questionable personal traits and given to the elevation of male favourites, this English king would soon alienate much of his nobility. Determined to keep down the unpopular costs of war (over and above the £100,000 or more of Italian banking debts he inherited from his father) and busy creating political crises at home this Edward would make only a token show of force in Scotland in 1307, withdrawing before the summer was out and not returning for three years. Crucially, this left the English occupation regime sorely undermanned and underpaid, dependent upon the ranks of Bruce's Scottish enemies to fill the gaps in their garrisons and to be their eyes and ears in the localities in the full knowledge that they could do little to aid these nobles in any fight.

Robert I seized this gaping window of opportunity with both hands, sparing himself and his men little. Risking a winter march north through mountainous passes the Bruce army penetrated the Great Glen. There, the striking absence of co-ordinating leadership either from England or John Comyn, Earl of Buchan (whose failure was thus as complete as in 1296), allowed Robert to isolate his opponents one-by-one, pass-by-pass, tower-by-tower. The impression that Bruce was a winner on the beginning of a roll began to take effect. The castles of Inverlochy, Urquhart and Invernairn fell 'by deceit and the treason of the men inside': as with all strongholds taken by Bruce's men these castles were then razed to the ground. By November 1307 William, Earl of Ross, had been forced to seek a private ceasefire and could only complain to Edward II that:

> 'we heard of the coming of sir Robert Bruce towards the parts of Ross with a great power, so that we had no power against him, but nevertheless we caused our men to be called out... Bruce would have destroyed them utterly if we had made no truce with him'.

From Ross, Robert I pressed on, destroying minor baronial castles in his path, to his first clash on Comyn lands near Elgin by the year's close.

His exertions had taken a heavy toll and Robert was periodically confined to a litter. But the new campaigning season of spring 1308 found him re-energised. At Inverurie on 23 May he scored his first decisive victory by routing 'a great many Scots and English' under the Earl of Buchan and Sir John Mowbray. But it was the manner in which this defeat of Bruce's greatest enemy was driven home which was most remarkable: for 'King Robert ravaged the earldom of Buchan with fire; and of the people, he killed whom he would, and to those whom he would have live, he granted life and peace'. This dreadful 'herschip' would still burn in the memory of north-eastern tenants unable to work their land fifty years later. Worse still, this savage action was echoed in the following summer by a similar assault in the south-west led by Robert's only surviving brother, Edward Bruce, with James Lindsay, Robert Boyd and James Douglas, who defeated the

14. Inverlochy Castle, Lochaber.
This was one of the key northern castles taken by Bruce from the Comyns and their party in 1307–8 and then destroyed: the Comyns really had no response to this style of warfare.

MacCans and 'slew many of the gentry of Galloway, and made nearly all the district subject to them. Those Gallovidians who could escape came to England to find refuge'. By the end of the year the Earl of Buchan was dead.

In June or July 1308 the vital North-Sea port of Aberdeen fell to the Bruce Scots. But for the moment Robert seemed little interested in the outside world. Marching back west in August he forced Alexander Macdougall of Argyll to surrender Dunstaffnage Castle and flee to England after a brilliant outflanking movement by Bruce's allies, the MacDonalds, at the pass of Brander. Anguished letters written in the previous spring from Argyll's son, John Macdougall of Lorn, to Edward II warning that he was 'not sure of my neighbours in any direction' underline the degree to which Bruce was thus able to play upon

15. Robert I's seal.
As King Robert could use patronage and parliament to legitimise his authority after usurping the throne. His first parliament was at St Andrews in March 1309: thereafter he began a redistribution of lands and offices in earnest.

intense local rivalries in destroying the Comyns' in-laws. In the face of such a collapse the Earl of Ross had no option but to submit finally in October 1308: the English garrison at Forfar fell in December to inspired townsmen.

However, such was Robert's need for support and further legitimisation that he knew he could never afford to destroy all his opponents. But of course as king not only could Robert issue pardons, he could also extend patronage to both his proven and potential followers by plundering the captured lands of his irreconcilable enemies as he went. In the first few years of Robert's reign such acts of favour may have been few, limited both by the need to issue grants which would motivate men to then go out and seize that territory from Balliol/Comyn party possession or English occupation; and by the cold fact that very few Scots may have been willing to accept charters from a usurper king not sure of retaining his throne. However, between 1309 and 1312, Robert would well and truly set the ball of resettlement rolling by granting Edward

16. *Galloglas* warriors of west Scotland.
Bruce was able to call upon the vital support of these kind of troops under
the MacDonalds of Islay, MacRuaridhs of Garmoran and Campbells of
Lochawe in fighting the Macdougalls and in invading Ireland.

Bruce the lordship of Galloway and by assigning the massive
regality of the earldom of Moray (embracing Badenoch and
Lochaber) to Sir Thomas Randolph, a Dumfriesshire knight and
Bruce's cousin: as with many of Robert's early grants these were
given in return for specific military services. In addition, Robert
filled key government offices, appointing Sir Robert Keith as the
Marishcal and Sir Gilbert Hay of Erroll as Constable (now that the
new Strathbogie Earl of Atholl had sided with England):
sheriffdoms and other administrative posts were also filled often in
advance of the expansion of Bruce geographical control.

These tentative beginnings of consolidation were also marked by
Robert's first parliament in mid-March 1309 held in the newly
captured cathedral burgh of St Andrews. Here Robert and his
closest advisors took extreme care to project an impression of
widespread community approval of the new regime. Declarations
were issued in the name of both the 'bishops, abbots, priors and
others of the clergy duly constituted in the realm of Scotland' and

of the noble 'inhabitants of the whole realm of Scotland acknowledging allegiance to king Robert'. The first of these statements was designed to refute the failure of the papacy (now based in Avignon) to recognise Robert's royal authority because he was an excommunicated murderer and usurper: remarkably, not only did this missive assert that the Scottish clergy recognised that Bruce was the rightful heir to Alexander III but it denounced John Balliol as an imposition of Edward I. The second declaration purported to be the response of Scotland's nobles to the request of the current French king, Philip V, that they join him on crusade: the subscribers thanked Philip both for his invitation (which they insisted they would only take up once the realm was secure) and for his limited recognition of 'the lord Robert... who has been raised up as our leader and prince' (highly significant as it came from the keeper of John Balliol and brother-in-law of Edward II).

In reality, however, this united front in parliament was an orchestrated sham. Recent research has shown that many of the bishops', earls' and lords' seals attached to these declarations belonged to individuals who were either dead, faithful to the English or, at best, of uncertain loyalty: many had clearly been coerced. The Bruce party had long since recognised the value of such propaganda, beginning in 1290–91 and expanding in scope as the civil war erupted in earnest. As early as May 1307, one Englishmen in Scotland had recorded how 'Bruce never had the good will of his own followers or of the people generally so much with him as now. It appears that God is with him... the people believe that Bruce will carry all before him, encouraged by false preachers from Bruce's army'. Many (but by no means all) clerics anxious to back the only man likely to revive an independent Scottish Crown and Church now likened war against the English to a holy crusade and even recounted Arthurian predictions that the inhabitants of Scotland and Wales would unite to destroy 'the covetous king' of England.

For now, though, there was little real danger that Bruce would swallow his own spin. He knew there remained much work to do. But if the vital tasks of asserting his authority in Scotland and completing his revolution at the level of local lordship could be taken in hand after March 1309 then he could look in turn to allowing his captains to take the war to England.

2

THE TRIUMPHANT ROAD TO BANNOCKBURN, 1310–14

'From the faces of two or three Scots, a hundred
English would flee'.
Thomas Walsingham, *Historia Anglicana*.

By 1310, the Bruce Scots were in control of north-eastern and much of western Scotland. However, Robert's conquest might be all too quickly undone if the English and Balliol Scots could break out once more from their frontier of garrisons north of the Forth at Dundee, Perth and Stirling and the core of their power in the south-east and south-west, from Edinburgh to Berwick and across to Roxburgh, Lochmaben and Caerlaverock. Moreover, this anti-Bruce coalition still contained significant Scottish landowners like David Strathbogie, Earl of Atholl; Malise, Earl of Strathearn; Patrick Dunbar, Earl of March; Duncan, Earl of Fife; Sir Adam Gordon; the Soules; Umphravilles; Barclays; Abernethys; Mowbrays; Macdougalls; Macdowells; MacCans and Macsweens as well as the few remaining Comyn scions: these lords could raise substantial regional followings.

All this meant that when Edward II finally decided to put in a military appearance in autumn 1310 Robert had to play a dangerous game. He was helped by the fact that Edward had really come to Scotland to take shelter with his current favourite, Piers Gaveston, from the political criticism of many of his own nobles. As a result, Edward's six-month campaign had very limited objectives: to bolster the southern garrisons of the occupation regime and give some succour to those bases besieged at the edge of English power like Dundee. But he could not offer his Scottish supporters any hope of aid or gains in real terms. Nonetheless, despite Edward's unpopularity, the Bruce Scots declined to engage his forces. Adopting the classic guerrilla tactic of withdrawing to high ground and scorching the earth to deny the enemy supply, Robert only emerged to snap at Edward's heels as he withdrew to England in July 1311 returning south to a storm in parliament at Westminster controlled by his baronial opponents, the Ordainers.

The failure of this expensive English campaign was, then, another turning point. With Edward II distracted by a domestic clash which would turn into his own civil war by 1312 (with Gaveston murdered in August that year), Robert and his lieutenants were free to concentrate on clearing central and much of southern Scotland of enemy garrisons and landlords. There followed over the next three years an incredible track record of success for the Bruce Scots in seizing many formidable royal burghs and castles by stealth, forcing the Scots inside to submit, sending the English home and then razing the strongholds' walls to the ground (saving the expense of repair and their own garrison as well as denying it to the enemy).

In this campaign Robert I led the way bravely, for example, wading across the icy moat at Perth in January 1313 to be the first up the scaling ladder and over the walls. Bruce's generals, too, made a name for themselves in their exploits with Douglas overwhelming Roxburgh Castle in early 1314 just a few weeks before Randolph overran Edinburgh. Such was the Bruce momentum on this home-front that by spring 1314 only the hugely symbolic garrisons of Stirling, Berwick and a few border castles held out. With little sign of a reply from Edward II, many Balliol Scots decided to defect in the face of duress and threat to their lands, including Atholl, Strathearn and Sir John Menteith: Bruce, still in search of support, reinstated them or their heirs.

Others like Patrick, Earl of March, purchased private truces on the borders to spare their lands from Bruce attack.

However, this tactic of selling periodic respite to his enemies was one which Bruce managed to export to devastating effect after July 1310. Between 1311 and 1314 the king and his lieutenants undertook the first in a series of systematic raids into the three northern English counties. Deploying small mounted divisions the Scots typically penetrated Northumberland and swept across and round in ever-increasing horseshoe-shaped raids through the wealthy bishop's palatinate of Durham, through Cumberland and parts of Westmorland or the duchy of Lancaster and back across the marches to Scotland.

In the long-term, the aim of these attacks, of only a few days' or at most weeks' duration, was to scare Edward II into recognising Bruce as king of a sovereign Scotland. But in the short-term – although there was the opportunity to target some lands belonging to nobles who had claimed Scottish lands in 1306 – the primary goal was economic. By isolating and granting individual English shires or religious institutions truces for six months or so at a time Robert not only ensured that his war effort became self-funding: he also gave indirect patronage through booty to his chief supporters, especially the triumvirate of Edward Bruce, Douglas and Randolph and their followers. In this manner it has been estimated that Bruce and his men earned more than £20,000 over the next decade. But this is surely to underestimate the wealth stolen by his troops. For if tribute was not forthcoming from an English region or lord the Scots would be back on the dot to burn, loot or rustle whatever they could get. Well-informed through spies and thus timed to coincide with harvests and English political crises these terrifying raids quickly denuded much of northern England and began to penetrate into Yorkshire: the Scots were always careful to guarantee passage through one region at truce so as to access unscathed lands further south. In the fluid zone of loyalties which was the shifting Anglo-Scottish border, many men increasingly did not care whether or not Bruce was king of Scotland: some began to defect from an Edwardian regime which could clearly not protect them.

By 1313–4, then, the Bruce Scots undeniably controlled the military initiative. Even though starving Anglo-Balliol garrisons in

Scotland and the three northern English counties were far remote from Westminster, Edward II could not afford to ignore for too long the threat to his inherited empire. The catalyst for his second campaign, however, was a measure of just how far Robert I's cause had advanced since 1306. For probably at a parliament at Cambuskenneth in October 1313, Robert threw down a final gauntlet to his Scottish opponents by demanding that they come into his peace within a year or face irreversible forfeiture of their lands. The occasion of Edward's decision to defend his Scottish supporters in the face of this Bruce ultimatum would, of course, be his attempt to relieve the siege of Stirling Castle in mid-summer 1314.

According to tradition, Edward Bruce had foolishly granted the Stirling garrison a countdown to surrender; they could only escape unless an English army came within three miles of its walls in relief. But in truth, Robert I (like Wallace in 1298) need not have given battle when Edward II and an army of at least 15,000 men did just that. However, Robert's excellent tactical use of the ground along the Torwood road from Edinburgh to Stirling on the first day of conflict, 23 June, exposed the indiscipline and weaknesses of the English host. Early skirmish victories for Robert's divisions and the king's own personal combat triumph in killing Henry de Bohun (nephew of one of only three earls in Edward's army) gave Bruce confidence: this was further boosted by the reports of the poor state of Edward's force given by Scots like Sir Alexander Seton who chose that night to change sides. The outcome, of course, was still not guaranteed: at least one Scot, the Strathbogie Earl of Atholl, defected the other way and the next day would sack Robert's baggage train. But Atholl could do nothing on 24 June as the English cavalry, archers and infantry, trapped by the Scots amidst the marshy streams of the Bannock Burn, were overwhelmed by Bruce spearmen:

> 'when both armies engaged each other, and the great horse of the English charged the pikes of the Scots, like into a dense forest, there arose a great and terrible clash of spears broken and of horses wounded to death... in confusion, many nobles and others fell into [the burn] with their mounts in the crush, while others escaped with much difficulty, and many were never able to extricate themselves from the ditch'.

17. The battle of Bannockburn, 1314.
This famous victory, beginning with Bruce's combat with the English knight, Henry de Bohun, failed to win the war with Edward II but signalled a real turning point in Bruce's struggle with his Scottish opponents.

Bruce's most celebrated triumph was, nonetheless, a missed opportunity to end the war with England in an instant because Edward II, aided by Patrick, Earl of March, was able to escape. The Scots' coffers were filled by the capture of the English baggage train but the real victory of that day was the defeat of many Balliol/Comyn Scots in English pay: some, like David Comyn of Kilbride and John Comyn, claimant of Badenoch, had been slain. True to his word, in a parliament at Cambuskenneth Abbey in November 1314, Robert would thus be able to deprive his enemies of their Scottish lands in a general statute of forfeiture. Men like the Earls of Dunbar and Fife, William Soules of Liddesdale, Sir Adam Gordon, David Barclay of Brechin and Ingelram d'Umphraville (some of them captured at Bannockburn) now decided to enter Robert's peace before it really was too late. They were encouraged to do so by the fact that the Bruce king was still sufficiently anxious for support as to pardon such men after the deadline and because there did now seem to be absolutely no hope of a Balliol restoration: not only had Edward II been humiliated but by late 1314 John Balliol had died, an old man in his seventies in exile on his estates in France. It had been a great year for Bruce.

3

IRELAND, THE SUCCESSION
AND TREASON, 1315–20

'…no-one be a conspirator nor inventor of tales or
rumours through which matter of discord may spring
between the lord king and his people'.
                    Act of Parliament of Scotland, December 1318.

With his cause thus blessed by God with victory in battle, Robert
I looked to the decisive consolidation of his dynastic authority. As
well as stepping up his redistribution of lands and offices to ensure
support for his regime the king had, above all, to provide for his
succession. In late 1314, the exchange of his queen, Elizabeth de
Burgh, their daughter, Marjorie, and other Bruce prisoners for
English lords captured at Bannockburn made this possible. The fact
that Robert would only be involved in person in one major raid
into northern England between 1314 and 1322 might be taken as
proof that he was determined to devote his energies to his domestic
rule. But Robert would not lose sight of the need to force Edward
II to the negotiating table. Bruce's pursuit of English recognition of

18. Cambuskenneth Abbey, Stirling.
Here, in 1304, Bruce had concluded a secret pact with Bishop Lamberton of St Andrews
to revive the kingship: in November 1314, Robert I followed up his victory at nearby
Bannockburn by forfeiting his enemies, as he had promised.

his sovereignty would involve him in another, even more dangerous theatre of war: the Scottish invasion of Ireland (1315–8).

Robert's patronage to his supporters after the mandate of Bannockburn intensified and did indeed amount to a revolution of local and regional lordship. Although the nobles who thus emerged as the leading lords of the kingdom throughout the fourteenth century were by no means 'new men' they were not the kindreds who would logically have prospered under a Balliol king or Comyn administration. It was the vast provincial titles and associated holdings of that displaced group (the Balliols, the Comyns and Macdougalls and others) as well as the many scattered territories acquired before 1286 now lost by aristocratic families based in England (like Guines, Zouche, Ferrers, Percy, Wake and Beaumont) which gave Bruce such scope to redraw the political map. The main beneficiaries of Robert's largesse continued to be the big three or four, his generals Edward Bruce, Randolph, Douglas and now Walter Steward (his father, James, having died in 1309) who in April 1315 was betrothed to the king's daughter, Marjorie. But other families would be similarly enriched and given the responsibility of policing the Bruce's former enemies in particular corners of the realm. It must be realised that very often it still remained for Bruce's followers to use force to place themselves in possession of their new lands (especially in cases where nobles prominent in one shire were to be planted in another).

In the far north and north-east, the Earl of Ross was granted much of Buchan and served alongside lesser families like the Keiths, Hays, Frasers and Chalmers. In Tayside and the ancient earldoms of Mar, Angus, Fife, Atholl, Menteith and Strathearn, Robert I looked to similar kindreds like the Ramsays, Campbells, Stewarts of Bonkil (from Berwickshire), Menteiths of Knapdale, Menzies of Fortingall and Malcolm, Earl of Lennox, to take control: the incumbent earls − either exiles or former Balliol men only recently admitted to the Bruce peace − were thus forced to abandon or promise their lands to Crown men by written entail. In the Lothians and south-east many lesser nobles and their kin were rewarded alongside James Douglas and other Crown familiars, although Sir Alexander Seton fared best. In Lanarkshire, Dumbartonshire and Ayrshire further local kindreds were raised under the Stewarts, the Boyds and the traditional Bruce followers of Carrick: many of these men also received land in Roxburghshire and elsewhere in the borders. Overall, together with Robert's marked favour between 1315 and 1320 to the monastic houses and dioceses of that most influential institution, the Scottish Church, as well as the recovering burghs, this was the beginning of a comprehensive resettlement overseen by an efficient Crown bureaucracy headed by Chancellor Bernard, Abbot of Arbroath. Significantly, it was only in the former Balliol-Comyn heartlands of Galloway and Wigtown that the Bruce regime was unable to advance its lordship before 1319.

Robert's problems in this latter region, however, were undoubtedly due to the necessary absence from the realm after May 1315 of his brother, Edward Bruce, Lord of Galloway and Earl of Carrick. Edward was a vital figure to the king not merely as a general and companion but as a means of off-setting mounting fears about the stability of the dynasty. As yet Robert was without a son of his own. Thus at a parliament in Ayr in April 1315 an Act of Succession was issued for the sake of avoiding a repeat of the chaos which had ensued after the Maid of Norway's inheritance in 1286. This statute recognised Edward Bruce and his legitimate male heirs as the royal heirs presumptive before Marjorie Bruce: Randolph was named as Guardian in the event of the deaths of all the adult heirs. Again the attachment of nobles' and prelates' seals to such a landmark document was a strict test of loyalty (of dubious legality as in displacing Marjorie it also threatened any future noble inheritance through a female line). But this contingency had also been laid because it had already been decided that Edward Bruce would lead a Scottish army west in an attempt to secure the kingship of Ireland.

The reasons for opening this second front (often neglected by Scottish historians) were many. Raids into northern England in late 1314 had not brought Edward II to the negotiating table and the extra pressure on his unpopular colonial regime in Ireland might force him to talk. That said, such a campaign would also stretch Bruce resources. Yet the possibility of lighting the touchpaper of native Irish resentment against Plantagenet imperialism (and, perhaps, the spread of such revolt to Wales) could forge a Pan-Celtic alliance against England.

But in addition it can be argued that the Bruce descent on Ireland was an extension of the personal feuds and Scottish civil war of 1306–14. In doing so the Bruce brothers could not only hunt down former enemies like the Macdougalls (captains of Edward's navy in the Irish sea) and the Macdowells (captains of the Isle of Man which the Bruces had attacked to secure for Randolph as early as 1313): but the Bruces could also reward their west-coast allies in this conflict, the MacDonalds and MacRuaridhs, and aid those who had sustained them in the winter of 1306–7 (the 1315 landing in Ulster did coincide with a Bruce galley attack on the Hebrides). The Bruces may even have been motivated to claim what they perceived as their Ulster inheritance by right of Robert's wife whose father, the 'red' earl, had aided England *c*.1299–1304. At the very least, the Scots might secure their western seaboard approaches and disrupt the supply of Irish grain, horses and troops to the English garrison town of Carlisle (which was also besieged by the Scots in summer 1315). Finally, of course, the Scots were on an invincible high after Bannockburn and ambitious men like Edward Bruce had to be kept sweet through conquest.

Robert I clearly viewed the collective weight of these reasons as compelling. Along with Thomas Randolph, Lord of Annandale, Nithsdale and Man as well as Earl of Moray, by 1318 the king would take part in three gruelling campaigns to aid his brother in Ireland. Although these sorties were timed to coincide with truces on the Anglo-Scottish border, allowing each front to be pushed in turn, the childless Robert nevertheless risked everything by participating. When the Scots' initial invasion failed to conquer land beyond Ulster in 1315–6, and quickly became bogged down in the unpredictable native rivalries of the Gaelic Irish, the Scots found themselves in the same rut as the English in attempting to overrun a divided Scotland. Unable to risk besieging Dublin the Scots instead launched raids to probe southern Ireland. Here in the winter of 1317, Robert, his brother and Randolph (the king, heir presumptive and would-be Guardian of Scotland) and their army so nearly perished from hunger. They achieved nothing.

Edward Bruce, then, had been made high king of Ireland in the summer of 1316 but he would never enjoy the power of this title. When James Douglas and others captured the town and castle of Berwick in April 1318, and Robert I determined to keep it, the Irish front stagnated. Frustrated, Edward led out his Ulster army on his own in autumn 1318. But on 14 October 1318 at Fochart near

19. Tomb of Angus Og MacDonald (d. 1318).
Angus – who fought for Bruce in 1314 – perished alongside Edward
Bruce in Ireland in 1318 and had been motivated to fight by the
opportunity to attack the Macdougalls and expand his kindred's
influence throughout the Irish Sea world.

Dundalk he was defeated and killed (along with MacDonald and
MacRuaridh heirs) by English forces. This disaster precipitated a
major crisis for the Bruce resettlement and dynasty. For almost as
soon as word reached England of the Scots' defeat, Edward II had
sent to France for Edward Balliol (who had taken up his father's
lands there in 1315). The English king and the rightful claimant to
the Scottish throne now rightly sensed Robert Bruce's great
vulnerability. Accordingly they contacted former Balliol Scots in
Robert's peace who were disgruntled and personally snubbed by his

regime's redistribution of lands and offices since 1314: men like Soules of Liddesdale, Umphraville (heir to Angus), Barclay of Brechin and perhaps the Comyn in-laws, the Earls of Strathearn, Fife and March as well as several key churchmen. Together with the disinherited Scots in exile – Atholl, Mar and the Macdougalls – this potentially large group was proof that the civil war was not yet over.

For his part, Robert I was also painfully aware of the danger unleashed by his brother's death. Thus at a parliament in Scone in December 1318 he attempted to shore up his authority (shortly after overseeing the consecration of the completed cathedral of Scotland's patron saint, Andrew). Another Act of Succession was passed for unquestioned sealing by his subjects this time recognising Robert's grandson, Robert Stewart (born in early 1316), as a stop-gap royal heir presumptive until Bruce had sons. But such was the threat sensed that Robert's regime also issued statutes ordering weapons practice and (quoted above) outlawing sedition and rumour-mongering against the Crown. Bruce was wise to be paranoid. Edward II was more interested at first in an armed expedition to recover Berwick which Robert had given in charge to Walter Steward and others. But when this English relief army collapsed in September 1319 in the face of Edward's squabbles with the Earl of Lancaster and crafty Scottish counter-raids (which very nearly captured the English king) underhand methods became a natural resort.

It was, then, a plot by former Balliol men in Scotland to assassinate Robert and usher in a Balliol coup which was discovered in summer 1320. Bruce may have further antagonised his former enemies in Scotland by attempting to build up Sir James Douglas's lands as the Crown agent in the south-west (where Soules and some of his confederates had their lands). Many Scots must also have been angered by another round of seal abuse and coercion by the royal government in demanding that nobles approve the Declaration of Arbroath to send to the papacy about 6 April 1320.

Yet in the end, it should not be forgotten that this plot was exposed by former Balliol Scots anxious to benefit from Bruce's patronage resettlement: men like Murdoch, claimant to the earldom of Menteith, and Patrick Dunbar, Earl of March, warned the king in hope of reward. Robert I, however, was understandably anxious to play down the Balliol dynastic threat this conspiracy posed. At the so-called 'Black Parliament' in August 1320 in which the conspirators were tried (and for which no official record survives) Robert made a cruel example of those involved. He gaoled Soules, Umphraville and the Countess of Strathearn and executed Barclay of Brechin for being complicit with the plot but not warning the Crown. Several other minor figures were condemned for their direct guilt and executed by being drawn by horses, a gory measure of Bruce's anger: this included Sir John Logie of Logie and Strath Gartney in Strathearn and Menteith respectively. Sir Roger Mowbray, whose lands were scattered about central and southern Scotland and who had died in skirmishes before he could be tried, was presented as a corpse for judgement. In the end, only a handful of those suspected – including Eustace Maxwell of Caerlaverock and Hamelin de Troup, sheriff of Aberdeen – were pardoned. But Robert also took great trouble to make it seem as if Soules alone had aimed at the throne, trivialising Balliol's input: it was this propaganda version of the plot which reached later Scottish chroniclers.

Nonetheless, that the former patriotic party of 1296–1304 – now 'the disinherited' – remained a potent threat long after Bannockburn is underlined by the large number of Scots who sought refuge in England in 1320–1, fleeing Bruce justice. That figures like Ingelram d'Umphraville (and perhaps Soules himself) could escape south from gaol in Scotland suggests, too, that there persisted much latent sympathy for the Balliol cause: Soules and Umphraville seem to have died in England in 1321–2. In all, at least ten of the forty-four barons named as witnesses to the Declaration of Arbroath had been accused of plotting regicide just weeks later: many of those acquitted of conspiracy in 1320 hailed from the north-east, south-west and Fife, areas which – as we shall see – would come out in support of Edward Balliol's invasion in 1332.

That said, the plot had been well and truly smashed and Balliol now slinked back to France: the forfeited Scottish lands of the guilty were distributed to royal associates including the gift of the Soules' lordship of Liddesdale to the king's own bastard son, Robert of Clackmannan, and other lands to Robert Stewart, James Douglas and Melrose Abbey. But it was really little wonder that King Robert was grateful to be able to sit out and regroup during what remained of a two-year truce agreed with Edward II in December 1319.

4

IN SEARCH OF CLOSURE,
1320–27

'...our most valiant prince, king and lord, the lord Robert, who, in order that his people and his inheritance might be delivered out of the hands of enemies, cheerfully endured toil and fatigue, hunger and danger, like another Maccabeus or Joshua... yet if he should give up what he has begun, seeking to make us or our kingdom subject to the king of England or to the English, we would exert ourselves at once to drive him out as our enemy and as a subverter of his own right and ours, and we would make some other man who was able to defend us our king; for as long as a hundred of us remain alive, we will never on any conditions be subject to the lordship of the English. For we do not fight for glory, or riches, or honours, but for freedom alone, which no good man gives up except with his life.'

These now famous words from the Declaration of Arbroath of 6 April 1320 had been designed by Robert I's government to persuade Pope John XXII to drop his public censures of excommunication placed upon the sacrilegious murderer 'Robert de Brus' after the Scots had broken a papal-imposed truce on the Anglo-Scottish border in 1318 (when they captured Berwick): this letter also sought to offset the threat of wider interdict on ecclesiastical services in Scotland. But Robert really had no intention that his subjects should use this passage as a statement of contractual kingship. Instead, the insertion of a warning written on behalf of the Scottish nobility that a king of Scots in league with the English could be replaced by force was surely directed against Edward Balliol, who *was* then about to bring in the English. The Declaration was also a test of loyalty for the baronage of Scotland to Bruce.

In the end, the Declaration had no effect on the Pope who preferred to listen to Edward II's lawyers. However, since it was 'rediscovered' in the nineteenth century, the Declaration has been celebrated as a magnificent statement of Scottish national identity and patriotism. Yet back in the 1320s – after what had been as much if not more so two decades and more of factional war within Scotland as a struggle against a foreign invader – it is still doubtful if all or any of Bruce's subjects would have seen matters in these emotive and ethnic terms. Robert and his closest supporters (especially in the Church) realised that for them to ultimately justify their seizure of power and land from the Balliol king and his followers they would have to wrap themselves up in the language and mantle of acting for the greater good of the kingdom, labelling the former patriotic party as creatures of an English king who (as the Declaration claimed) burned Scottish churches, raped nuns and killed children. But it would take time, a return to normal, stable everyday life and the creation of a strong culture of vested interest under Bruce as king before the majority of Scots would transfer to Robert I the sense of identification of their own locality with one king, one nation and one Church which had first stirred under Alexanders II and III before 1286.

It followed, then, that Robert I worked even harder after August 1320 to secure and guarantee the stability of his realm and dynasty and the backing of a majority of Scots. He still had no son of his own: he was now forty-six (and perhaps already aware of the illness that would claim his life in 1329). Nor was Edward II any more likely to concede Scottish independence after the failures of the siege of Berwick and the Balliol plot.

In 1315 Robert I had insisted that he 'desired and still desires at all times to negotiate with the king of England on a final peace between them and us'. But in fact, both sides at first seemed committed to a resumption of the cross-border violence of 1311–19. When the two-year truce came to an end in December 1321, Robert and his lieutenants were ready to launch another raid, this time penetrating as far south as Richmond in Yorkshire again extracting tribute and valuable livestock. However, in reality, Robert may have decided on a change of tack, attempting to win the sympathy of influential English border lords as a prelude to pressing for a final peace and English recognition of his kingship. Accordingly, in early 1322, Robert granted a private truce to Sir Andrew Harcla, keeper of Carlisle, who had first made his name defending this vital strongpoint against Scottish assault in 1315. But that Robert had been prepared to do so may have been a revealing measure of just how anxious he was to secure a permanent peace. For Harcla was now free to raise an army to defeat the two great northern English rebels against his king, the Earls of Lancaster and Hereford, a fifth column the Bruce Scots may indeed have earlier tried to aid against Edward II. The destruction of these rebels at the battle of Boroughbridge on 16 March 1322 helped further consolidate Edward II's recovery of political power after the recurrent crises of the previous decade. Robert and Edward then agreed a truce to last until October 1322.

Yet if the Scottish king had expected such concessions to soften the English Crown to talk of peace between equals that summer would bring an English royal army north to Scotland for only the fourth time since 1307: this time, Edward II broke the truce. Ever alert, Robert's lieutenants launched a pre-emptive strike, raiding into north-western England as far as Preston while Edward went up the east coast to Edinburgh only to find that the Scots had stripped the land bare. Withdrawing south having achieved nothing Edward was nearly captured once again by the lurking Scots (who had been besieging Norham Castle): the English baggage train was taken once again at Bylands Abbey in Yorkshire.

By now Robert must have felt that the seizure of a royal prisoner was the only way he was going to use military force to make Edward negotiate. But in fact the cumulative failure of another Edwardian campaign and Scottish retaliation had been enough to

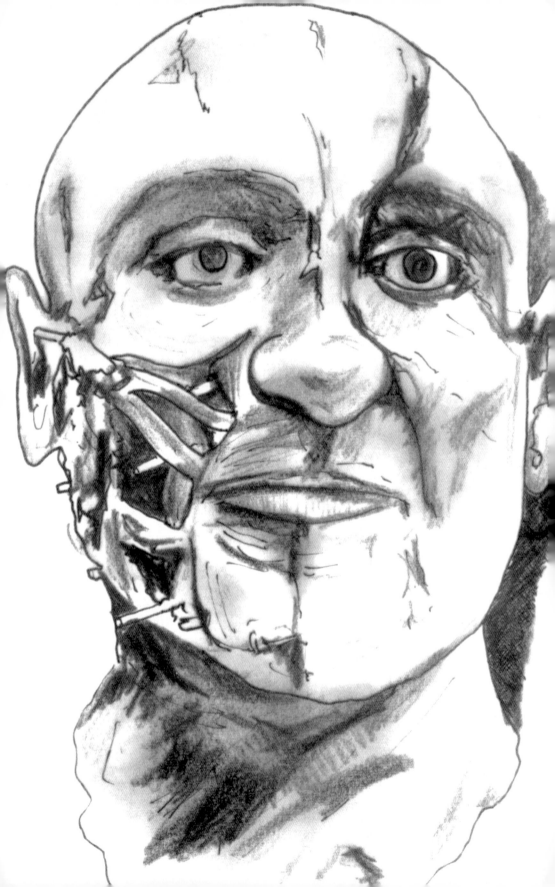

convince Andrew Harcla (now Earl of Carlisle) that the English king was incapable of defending the northern border. In January 1323 this border lord thus accepted private peace terms offered by Robert I (which may thus have been on the table for some time). By the terms of this treaty it was agreed that England and Scotland were to be separate kingdoms with their own kings, customs and laws; to settle future border disputes each side would name six arbiters to act in concert; and if either Bruce or Harcla were obliged to take an army into the opposing realm they promised not to damage each other's lands and goods. Moreover, Harcla promised that he would try and persuade Edward II to accept a general peace. If he did so within a year, Robert would pay the English 40,000 merks (about £27,000) in war damages and establish a monastery endowed with 500 merks a year to say Masses for the war dead: he would also allow the English king the right to choose a wife for Robert's male heir, at that time his grandson Robert Stewart. Finally, neither king was to restore their forfeited opponents to their former lands in each other's realms – there was to be no return to the cross-border landholding of pre-1286.

A number of these clauses are especially interesting. So anxious for peace was Robert that he had offered reparations and a royal wedding to the English, the latter suggesting a desire to return to the inter-marriage of the thirteenth century as a means of guaranteeing amicable relations. But the adamant rejection of the 'disinherited' – those Scottish noble families forfeited of their lands since 1314, a group which by now also included a number of influential English families who had fallen heir by marriage to Scottish lines killed off by Bruce – was clear proof that Robert was aware that they were a grave threat to his careful redistribution of land and offices as a means of winning support after 1306.

As such, the outcome of the Scottish civil war threatened to sabotage any peace with England. Overall, it was perhaps naïve of Robert and his council to expect Edward II to accept such terms and the end of his claim to Scotland. As it was, the troubled English king flew into a rage characteristic of his father and

Opposite Page: 20. The face of a hero?
Based upon the skull excavated from Dunfermline Abbey in 1819 this reconstruction shows the war wounds and disease from which Bruce suffered in his later years.

executed Harcla. It is possible that this was what Robert had hoped for all along, the removal of the one effective defender of the north. Yet not only would these 1323 terms form the basis of the final conditions for peace dictated by Robert four years later; but within just a few weeks, by May 1323, the Bruce Scots had concluded a remarkable thirteen-year truce with Edward II. This was an admission by Robert that the war was going nowhere and he needed a breathing space to continue rebuilding his kingdom and stabilising his dynasty.

Indeed, it is tempting to speculate that the birth of David Bruce about nine months later at Dunfermline on 5 March 1324 (and perhaps a twin son, John, who died in infancy) was related directly to the conclusion of this long ceasefire which in turn guaranteed no more Scottish interference in Ulster and Ireland (the home of Robert's queen)! But the birth of a son was undoubtedly a joyous event for Bruce. It came in the middle of a decade which saw Robert issue by far the majority of his acts of patronage as king. In particular, the mid-to-late 1320s saw much of his favour to Alexander Seton in the Lothians alongside Sir Robert Lauder of the Bass, justiciar of that region; Robert Keith and his kin; the Douglases of Lothian as well as the 'good' Sir James Douglas (who was given the Balliol lordship of Buittle in 1325); Sir Andrew Murray of Bothwell, son of Wallace's companion of 1297 and husband of Robert's sister, Christian, who had been granted the lordship of Garioch adjacent to Mar by 1326; extra lands and office responsibilities for Randolph; the vast northern Strathbogie lordship to the former Comyn man, Sir Adam Gordon; Lothian and Roxburghshire lands for Robert Steward (after the death of his father, Walter, in 1327); as well as extensive favour for the abbeys of Melrose, Dunfermline and Arbroath and the priory of Whithorn in Galloway. The late 1320s may also have seen the king grant (by acts now lost) the forfeit earldoms of Angus and Menteith to the Stewarts of Bonkil and John, the son of Neil Campbell of Lochaw and his wife, Mary Bruce, respectively: under the terms of Earl Duncan of Fife's submission to Bruce of 1315 the king may also have been able to assign the premier earldom of Fife to Robert Steward.

These and Robert I's hundreds of other minor acts of 'alienation' of royal lands and revenues, often in return for military services, meant that by July 1326 the king was obliged to ask his

21. Braveheart Bruce?
Undoubtedly inspired by a certain film as well as by Barbour's words from
The Bruce, this stone was laid in 2001 to mark the spot of Bruce's
embalmed heart before the high altar at Melrose Abbey.

subjects for taxation to help sustain his household. Parliament duly
granted the king a tenth of all land rents for life, an apparently
grateful concession which suggests that Bruce was firmly in control
of his subjects by that date. However, the huge drain on Crown
resources through patronage – and Robert's extensive gifts of land
often with rights of jurisdiction autonomous from the Crown (in
'free barony' or 'regality') – has drawn some historians to argue that
in the long-term this policy contributed to the dangerous

undermining of royal authority. In the course of his revolution Robert had had to reward well to get support: but he created potentially overmighty magnates in the localities along the way.

Some slight evidence of tension between king and great regional magnates can be detected in the period c.1320–9: the MacRuaridhs had to be forfeited by the Crown in parliament in 1325 and Sir James Douglas, the MacDonalds and the Earl of Ross seemed keen to be left alone to control resources and men in the south, west and far north. It would have been quite natural, too, for some of Robert's ambitious young nobles to have been jealous over just who emerged with the rank of earl. Ultimately, the grave problems of authority which David Bruce would encounter as king in clashing with the various houses of Stewart, Douglas, March and Ross after 1341 certainly suggests that Robert I may have been fortunate to die before the honeymoon period of his support was over and he suddenly found himself bereft of resources and surrounded with hungry and feuding noble scions.

However, in 1326 this legacy lay in the uncertain future. To further determine the path the years ahead would take, the king also used the parliament of July 1326 to require his prelates and nobles to attach their seals to a third act of succession, this time recognising David Bruce as heir to the throne ahead of Robert Stewart with the government of either minor king to be overseen in the event of Robert I's death by Randolph then Douglas as Regent. In addition, parliament – including representatives of the Scottish royal burghs – ratified a new treaty of alliance with France which had been negotiated at Corbeil by October 1325 by an embassy including Bishop Lamberton of St Andrews, Andrew Murray the Bishop of Brechin, Sir Robert Keith and Randolph (who had also had some success in Avignon in 1324 in smoothing papal attitudes to Bruce and his regime). As we shall see, together with Robert's ongoing resettlement programme, these parliamentary acts would prove to be the vital pillars upon which the Bruce monarchy of an independent Scotland would survive after 1329.

Nevertheless, that Robert felt them so vital in 1326 betrayed his grave concerns for what might come to pass. As the king was now probably failing in health, these contingencies also point to Robert's shrewd understanding that further war – both against England and the Bruces' Scottish enemies – would have to be fought.

5

UNFINISHED BUSINESS, 1327–29

'...accursede be the tyme that this parlement was ordeynede at Norhamton for there through false conseile the Kyng was there falsely disinherited.'

The Brut of the Chronicles of England

If there was another gift with which Robert Bruce was blessed – despite the hardships of 1306–7 – it was luck. In 1326–7, the fates conspired to bring him one last (perhaps not unexpected) chance to force England to recognise his kingship and Scottish independence: unlike in 1302, this time events outwith the kingdom favoured Scottish success and involved a last brief flurry of military activity which the ageing, ailing king of Scots must have relished.

For in September 1326, Edward II's queen, Isabella, returned from her brother's kingdom of France where she had negotiated an end to two years of Anglo-French conflict (1323–5). But she brought with her an ambitious lover, Roger Mortimer, and an army with which to challenge her husband and his new favourites, the Despensers. The resulting civil war in England, however brief, gave Bruce an opportunity to exploit English weakness. Before rumours that Edward II was even prepared to make massive

22. Sweetheart Abbey, Kirkcudbrightshire.
Built by King John's mother, Devorguilla, to hold the embalmed heart of her
Balliol husband (d. 1268) this shrine may have inspired Bruce to leave his
own memorial at Melrose.

concessions to Robert to secure his help could be substantiated, the deeply unpopular English king was arrested. By 20 January 1327 he had been deposed in favour of his fourteen-year-old son and namesake by the supposed authority of the clergy, magnates and people of the community of his realm in parliament: a little later he was brutally tortured to death. Now England, too, had an illegal usurper regime – of regicides to boot – in dire need of support and the means to legitimise itself. Understandably unable to prosecute war in the north, Isabella and Mortimer confirmed the truce with the Bruce Scots on the same day.

However, having experienced a similar political baptism Bruce saw his chance. On 2 February 1327, the very day of Edward III's coronation, the Scots broke the truce and attempted to take Norham Castle in a surprise attack. This opened an intense period of Scottish raiding to which the new English regime sought to reply by rallying troops to their standard for war against the Scots. In mid-June the Scots raided towards Durham while an English army under the new teenage king approached. Rather than simply scorch the earth in southern Scotland and evade conflict, a three-prong Scottish force sought to head off Edward III's first army (suggesting, perhaps, that Robert I was anxious to protect all that had been rebuilt between Roxburgh and Edinburgh since 1323). At Stanhope Park in northern Yorkshire the Scots' tactics paid off and the division of James Douglas – supported by those of Randolph and Donald, Earl of Mar (a follower of Edward II, finally returned north) – almost captured the English king scaring him to tears by attacking his tents in the night. The French chronicler, Jean le Bel, accompanying the English forces, has famously described how thereafter the elusive Scots, riding stocky ponies and travelling light with minimal supplies, led the arrayed chivalry-in-armour of the English host a merry dance around the moors. While all of this was happening, Robert I had again gone to Ulster, this time not to rouse the native Gaels but to brow-beat the steward of his wife's nephew's earldom of Ulster and extract supply therefrom.

This two-front Scottish campaign – a variation on Bruce's methods before 1318 – carried the day. Leaving Robert to begin besieging Norham once more in August, Isabella and Mortimer returned to London bankrupt and without having reached Scotland. They had to sue for peace. Now Robert could dictate his terms and at talks in Newcastle in late October 1327 he presented his demands. Crucially, these were much more favourable to the Scots than those offered to Harcla in 1323, if still very similar. Robert and his heirs as kings of Scots were to hold Scotland 'free and quit' of homage to England, a state of sovereignty which Edward III and his nobility must recognise formally; Prince David was to wed Edward III's sister, Joan; no subject of either king was to seek lands in the realm of the other, prohibiting a full restoration of the disinherited unless they gave up their English ties; a military alliance was to exist between England and Scotland against any potential enemy except the Scots' ally the French; the Scots would pay war damages of just £20,000 over three years; and, finally, the English were to undo their slander at Avignon and help get the papal excommunication upon Bruce lifted.

However, it was the legacy of fallout from the Scottish civil war which prevented these terms from simply being translated into a final peace treaty. A core group of the English heirs to disinherited Scots – headed by Sir Henry Beaumont, heir to the Comyn earldom of Buchan – had backed Isabella and Mortimer against Edward II, the king who had neglected the Balliol cause. As such the English queen-mother could not afford to ignore this powerful lobby and it is reasonable to infer that she and her ambassadors pressed for the inclusion of the disinherited in the peace deal with Scotland. Recent research, indeed, has shown that the final treaty of Edinburgh-Northampton of March–June 1328 may have included some promises for the restoration of these lords to their Scottish lands. A grant by Robert I to one of their number, Sir Henry Percy, given at Glasgow on 28 July, allowing him the right to pursue his father's lost Scottish lands (Urr in Galloway and Redcastle in Angus) in Bruce's courts suggests that these may have been private, selective concessions. Nonetheless, numerous letters of complaint written by Edward III to the Scots between 1329 and 1332 – insisting that they restore Percy, Beaumont and other nobles, as well as numerous English Church institutions, to their Scottish lands 'in accordance with the treaty' – underlines the fact that Robert had had to back down over this matter after October 1327 to get his peace and marriage alliance with England. The restoration by May 1329 of Sir James Douglas to his family's pre-1296 lands in England (and those of another Scot, Sir Henry Prendergast) also points to reciprocation on this matter by Isabella and Mortimer.

But the fact that the English would later complain so loudly makes it clear that Robert again changed his mind and fudged the issue of the disinherited. That he did so is understandable. The other peace terms he dearly wanted. He got his formal statement of renunciation of overlordship from Edward III and his subjects on 1 March 1328. The rest of the treaty was finalised solemnly *in Scotland* in a parliament at Holyrood Abbey outside Edinburgh two weeks later: the English then ratified it at a parliament in Northampton. The wedding of David and Joan – aged only four and seven a-piece – would go ahead by proxy (as the lawful age of marriage was fourteen for males, twelve for females) at Berwick on 12 July 1328: Joan was to get £2,000 worth of dower lands in

Scotland, a burden eased by the fact that the Scots were to retain all the territory they had recovered by 1318. The same Scottish parliament of 1328 also granted Robert's regime another tenth penny tax to help pay off the war damages by 1331 and a military alliance with England was declared against all enemies, saving the Scots treaty with France and with the stipulation that the Scots would not interfere in Ireland nor the English in the Isle of Man. Finally, the English did stand by their oath to help lift the excommunication, letters for which were issued by the Pope in October 1328 (reaching Scotland in July 1329).

Yet long before many of these clauses were brought to a successful closure Robert must have recoiled from the messy upheaval which the restoration of any of the disinherited might cause to his resettlement since 1314, especially the return of men like the Macdougalls, the Beaumont heir to Buchan or the Strathbogie Earl of Atholl. Bruce's close supporters simply would not tolerate the reduction of their new-found and hard-earned wealth and status. And Bruce himself knew that as much as David's betrothal and the £20,000 were means to bind the two realms in peace, any return to mutual cross-border land-holding would dilute his own authority and the growing corporate identity of the Scottish political community under his grip (even though he may have been tempted to recover the Bruce family's English lands). The revolution had simply gone too far to turn back.

The advisability of this Bruce retraction over the disinherited, though, may have been confirmed by the strained atmosphere of David's wedding in July where neither Edward III or Robert (who had paid over £1,000 for the celebrations) were present. Isabella and Mortimer may have taken this opportunity to negotiate with the Scots, perhaps attempting to extract concessions over Percy, Beaumont and others in return for extra pressure from the English government on the people of London who had refused riotously to allow the stone of Scone, brought south as a symbolic trophy by Edward I in 1296, to be removed from its place below the coronation chair in Westminster Abbey and returned north. But while the English were attempting to adjust the deal, the Scottish king was back in Ulster once more, not strictly interfering but 'helping' install his wife's nephew as earl. All in all, the second half of 1328 does give the impression that both sides were already jockeying for the upper hand and moral high ground in advance of future poor relations and conflict.

But by now Robert must have known he had only a short while to live. When in Ulster in 1327, the Anglo-Irish had reported to Isabella that Robert had been so sick he could only move his tongue to speak; at Holyrood in 1328 he apparently lay ill in an ante-chamber while the peace treaty was concluded. Whatever disease he had (which many English commentators assumed was leprosy), Robert had already withdrawn partly from public life, establishing a manor house at Cardross near Dumbarton. It was from here that he set out in early February 1329 on a last pilgrimage to the shrine of St Ninian at Whithorn in Galloway, one of several national and regional saints' cults observed by Bruce throughout his reign. But this was not merely a parting act of faith. During a journey which took some weeks Robert also took pains to visit much of Ayrshire, Carrick (stopping at his birthplace, Turnberry), Wigtown and Galloway and granted a number of acts to south-western and west coast natives in return for military services: in all he added the levy of two galleys, four armed men, four archers and a spearman to the potential host of the Crown.

In sum, Robert was adding to the defences of the realm in its most sensitive quarter, the heartland of both Bruce and Balliol-Comyn lands and a region his dynasty could not be sure to control (the Bruce regime had certainly established no sheriffs there after 1314). These preparations, together with Robert's ominous deathbed advice to his son and subjects never to fight a pitched battle, were a final admission that he perceived trouble ahead, the re-eruption of civil strife in Scotland at both local and national levels. Even Robert's funerary requests can be said to have reflected a need to guard against further war. For although his body was to be interred at Dunfermline Abbey alongside the remains of the royal he recognised as his immediate predecessor, Alexander III, Bruce's heart was to be taken to the Holy Land by his champion knight, Douglas, and then laid to rest in Melrose Abbey (his viscera were placed separately in a chapel near Cardross). Bruce's heart could thus serve as a warning to invading English armies (just as Edward I had planned to have his bleached bones carried high into battle against the Scots); but it might also rival the shrine of the heart of John Balliol's father at Sweetheart Abbey in Galloway.

23. Where do ex-kings go to die?
This plaque identifying a badly damaged knight's tomb in the church of St Waast in Bailleul-Neuville in Normandy is surely not that of the late king of Scots by that name (despite the claims of nineteenth-century French scholars).

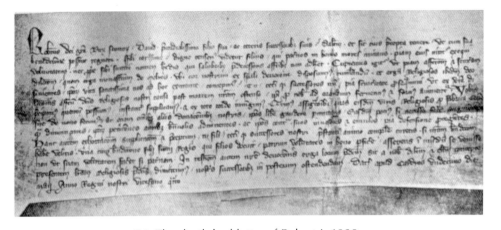

24. The death-bed letter of Robert I, 1329.
Bruce's funerary requests would be carried out to the letter but his son and subjects would not heed his warning not to fight pitched battles.

Yet at the end, despite these careful arrangements and the great political achievements of his last few years, when he passed away on 7 June 1329, aged fifty-five, Robert I can only have hoped that he had done enough for his infant successor to survive the unfinished business of his wartime generation.

PART THREE
A WAR
WON IN DEFEAT

1

THE RETURN OF BALLIOL,
1329-32

'Twynham Lourison… compelled to leave the kingdom and make for France… approached Edward Balliol and spoke with him as follows: "See my lord, king of Scotland, it is now time for you to reign; for the time is coming, and if you pass it by, you will be called the most unfortunate of men. See, Robert Bruce who occupied your kingdom is dead, and his son is a boy. Thomas Randolph the guardian of Scotland survives alone, for James de Douglas has set out for the Holy Land, and there is no one else who may be advanced to the kingship. If therefore you want to follow my advice, you will easily seize the sceptre of your kingdom. Have you not heard of the destruction of the nobility at the Black Parliament? Their families will stand by you; the king of England will provide a powerful force of armed men to help you. Hurry and get started; be of good heart, consult your friends, and take up arms."'

Walter Bower's *Scotichronicon*, c.1440

Scots like Lourison who had fled south in the wake of the brutal Black Parliament trial of the Soules conspiracy in 1320 would indeed have tried to encourage Edward Balliol and their English hosts to attempt another coup against Bruce. But in 1327–8 their voices had been lost amidst the squabbling of internal English politics and the peace treaty with Robert I and Scotland. The influential English lords who could claim Scottish lands – headed by Sir Henry Beaumont – preferred to attempt to bargain their way into the peace negotiations of Edinburgh-Northampton and almost pulled it off. At that time, they didn't need Edward Balliol or his exiled Scottish followers like the Strathbogie Earl of Atholl (the son-in-law of Beaumont), the Macdougalls, Macdowells, Mowbrays and Umphravilles. Hope for this group surely began to fade. It may have been about this time that Edward Balliol, now in his late forties and denied his full inheritance for all his adult life, took a wife in Margherita of Taranto, niece of the King of Naples and of Philip IV of France, and seemed set to live out his days on his Picardy estates.

However, the Scots' last-minute exclusion of the disinherited and the young Edward III's tearful disgust with what he saw as a 'shameful peace' and marriage for his sister in 1328 rendered Edward Balliol a valuable figurehead once more. With Robert Bruce's death and the succession of his five-year-old son as king this sense of opportunity must have doubled. By late 1329 Henry Beaumont and his associates were already in contact with Balliol, perhaps, as one English source suggests, liberating him from gaol in France for protecting one of his men from a charge of murder: it was about this time, too, that Balliol must have been persuaded to annul his marriage to his Italian wife. But the disinherited undoubtedly sounded Balliol out with a view to proposing a military expedition to Scotland backed by the English king.

In the end, though, this band had to wait almost three years for their day in the sun. Edward III did not break free from the control of his mother and execute the hated Mortimer until October 1330. Even then the English king needed time to stabilise his own

Opposite Page: 25. The tomb of Sir James Douglas (d. 1330),
St Bride's Church, Douglas
Killed while taking Bruce's heart on crusade, Douglas was a vital Scottish
general who had done much of the hard-work of recovering southern
Scotland from Bruce's Scottish enemies as well as the English: his death left
the Bruce Scots short of leaders at a crucial time.

authority at home and besides preferred to wait until the Scots had paid off the £20,000 war damages owed by autumn 1331. This must have been an extremely frustrating period for the disinherited and for Balliol: he remained in France until late 1331. Indeed, this long period of delay in breaking the Anglo-Scottish peace which had been negotiated by Isabella's illegal regime had seen the Bruce Scots further weakened. Not only did David's regency government hold off on his ceremonial installation as king until the reparations had been paid, but on 25 August 1330 Sir James Douglas was killed while fighting in Spain against the Saracens in the course of conveying Bruce's heart to the Holy Land. The loss of this able general – added to the deaths in turn of Walter Steward (1327), Bishop Lamberton of St Andrews (1328), King Robert (1329) and former Chancellor Bernard of Arbroath (1331) – must have given many in Scotland fear for the future stability of the Bruce regime and its land resettlement without its most able military and political leaders, especially as their child-king had not yet been crowned.

However, in Guardian Thomas Randolph, Earl of Moray, the Bruce Scots still had a pillar to support them. His period of governance, indeed, has long been praised by Scottish medieval chroniclers and modern historians alike as was one of remarkable stability. Praised for his attention to justice as a model for any king Randolph also ensured that the war damages were collected and paid on time and that the Scots did not waver on their decision to deny English demands to restore disinherited lands: he protected Scottish territorial rights passionately even going so far as to summon the Bishop of Durham to a Scottish parliament to answer for lands he claimed were his on the border. Only in his dealings with his fellow great magnates may Randolph have encountered some difficulty, for example in policing the racketeering by the Earl of Ross in the north (where the Guardian had to hang fifty wrongdoers) and, it seems, in recognising Alexander Bruce – an illegitimate son of Edward Bruce by the aunt of the current exiled Strathbogie Earl of Atholl – as Earl of Carrick: this last move perhaps upset the old king's grandson, Robert Steward, who feared his displacement from the royal succession by this royal cousin.

But on 24 November 1331, Randolph finally oversaw David II's solemn elevation as king at Scone, taking full advantage of the rite of coronation and unction (anointment with holy oil) which had been

Robert I's last achievement when granted by the papacy in 1329. Bearing a child-size crown, sceptre and orb, David (alongside his queen, Joan) was blessed by the new Bishop of St Andrews and gave his oaths to maintain the realm and its customs, laws and Church before a fully assembled parliament. The king was knighted along with several nobles' sons as his comrades, including Randolph's own namesake and heir and Thomas Stewart, son of the new Earl of Angus.

This should have been a splendid occasion of community support for the Bruce regime. However, the probable refusal to appear and perform their traditional role in these regal rites of Duncan, Earl of Fife, and Malise, Earl of Strathearn, may have dampened proceedings. Both these lords had been harshly treated by Robert I, Fife especially was forced to agree to the Crown's claim to reassign his earldom if he died without an heir at a time when he was separated from his English wife, a grand-daughter of Edward I. Other former Balliol/Comyn supporters, and even some staunch Bruce men, must also have doubted the wisdom of inaugurating a child-king when the rightful adult alternative was waiting in the wings, poised with an English army: perhaps it would be better to invite Balliol in as king without a fight, negotiating to safeguard or readdress the shift in territorial power effected since 1306.

Evidence that some Scots may indeed have felt this way would emerge over the next twelve months. But even to the coronation parliament it must have been clear that war was coming. By summer of 1332, indeed, Randolph was to be found in East Lothian preparing the realm's defences against anticipated attack from the south, so angry had Edward III's letters about the disinherited's snubbing by the Scots become. Word had surely reached the Bruce Scots, too, that Edward Balliol was in Yorkshire with his followers. But it was at this moment that a final thinning of the ranks of Robert I's generation struck a fatal blow to the Bruce Scots. On 20 July 1332 Thomas Randolph died at Musselburgh. He had probably been claimed by a long illness but the Scottish rumour of poison administered by a cleric in English pay should not be discounted. As underhand a method as the conspiracy of 1320, such an assassination left the Scots rudderless at a vital moment.

Now the necessity of choosing a new leader soon exposed division and doubt amongst the remaining Bruce Scots. According to the contemporary Scottish source of John of Fordun:

'all the magnates, both churchmen and laymen, were
gathered together at Perth on the 2nd of August
[1332]; and, after a great deal of wrangling and sundry
disputes, they, with one voice, chose Donald, earl of
Mar, as guardian of the kingdom'.

Mar may have been an equivocal choice to say the least. An
adherent of Edward II in England until 1327, Donald had had an
illegitimate child by a Balliol woman and is reported to have visited
Edward Balliol in England in 1331. One English chronicler,
indeed, asserts that he had told the pretender that:

'alle the grete lordes of Scotland shulde be to hem
entenant, and holde of him for thir Kyng, as right heir
of Scotland, and so miche thai wolde done, that he
shulde be crownde kyng of that lande, and to him dede
feaute and homage'.

Thus Mar's election as guardian in 1332 might have left the door
open for the Bruce Scots to negotiate with Balliol.

However, by 2 August, Balliol and the disinherited had already
made it clear that the time for talking had passed. On 31 July
Edward, Beaumont, Strathbogie, Gilbert d'Umphraville of Angus,
Sir Henry Percy, Thomas Wake of Liddel, Sir Alexander Mowbray,
Thomas Ferrers and a lone Comyn, Walter the claimant of
Kilbride, leading up to 2,000 or 3,000 seasoned troops, had arrived
in an armada of hired northern English ships in the firth of Forth.
They had no official Plantagenet support: Edward III could not be
seen to be the first to breach a papally sanctioned peace treaty. But
when on 6 August this invasion force came ashore at the royal
manor of Kinghorn in Fife (the site of Alexander III's death in
1286) all the old sores of the Bruce-Balliol civil war were re-
opened with devastating effect.

Perhaps taken aback that they were now to be attacked for their
reluctant submission to Bruce, the Earls of Fife and Mar (who was
also heir to the throne after Robert Steward) committed
themselves to fight off this invasion. The Guardian had superior
numbers by far as he marched to meet Balliol's force as it passed
through west Fife via Dunfermline towards Scone, guided by a

defector, Andrew Murray of Tullibardine. But when the enemy was confronted before Perth at Dupplin Muir on 11 August Earl Donald's leadership was most likely brought into question by the late king's bastard son, Robert Bruce of Clackmannan and Liddesdale, who accused him of treason. Thus unsettled the Scottish host inevitably suffered from poor generalship and fighting spirit. The resulting rout and victory for Balliol left a dreadful death-toll, claiming Mar; Murdoch, Earl of Menteith; Thomas Randolph (junior) the new Earl of Moray; Bruce of Liddesdale; Sir Alexander Fraser and many other valuable knights, perhaps 3,000–4,000 men in all.

With this blessing for his cause Edward Balliol now began to receive defectors *en masse*. In Galloway many of the native kindreds of that province rose in support of their rightful lord led by Sir Eustace Maxwell of Caerlaverock Castle (a man suspected of complicity in the plot of 1320): it was his armed following which successfully headed off a Perth-bound relief army raised from East Lothian by Patrick Dunbar, Earl of March (who may have helped betray the 1320 plot). At the same time, several lords from Aberdeenshire and Banffshire – the old Comyn heartlands – also revealed their true colours, including Hamelin de Troup, another suspect of 1320. Thus with the momentum for his campaign building in various regions Balliol also began to extract homage from the communities of central Scotland's ancient earldoms. The chivalry and clergy of Fife, Strathearn (including Perth) and Angus and the Mearns are said to have come over willingly: Earls Duncan and Malise were surely not too unhappy to blow with the prevailing wind. These two key magnates were certainly present and performed their ceremonial duties of investiture at Scone on 24 September 1332 when Balliol in turn was crowned king using his father's old gold coronet, sceptre and orb (which must have been released to him by the English monarchy): William Sinclair, Bishop of Dunkeld – head of the diocese extending from just north of Stirling into the earldom of Atholl and one of Robert I's fiercest supporters after 1314 – blessed the new Balliol monarch in the absence of Bishop Ben of St Andrews: he had already fled abroad. Even men like Alexander Bruce, Earl of Carrick, Robert Keith the Marischal, Sir Robert Lauder and Andrew Murray, Bishop of Brechin, may have been forced to submit to Balliol at this time.

26. Edward Balliol, Andrew Murray, Archibald Douglas, Randolph and the boy king, David II.
The prospect of a long Bruce minority was too good an opportunity for the middle-aged Balliol to miss after 1329: but he would meet stiff resistance from Scots well rewarded by Robert I.

The Bruce Scots were now staring down the barrel of defeat as the disinherited set themselves to recover their lands and more. However, it was precisely this vested interest in protecting their hard-won wealth and status which Robert I had counted upon motivating his men to sustain his dynasty. When Balliol took the remarkable step on 23 November 1332 of granting to Edward III most of the southern counties of Scotland – really the most valuable of the realm – the cold reality of the imminent dismemberment of the Bruce resettlement cannot have failed to strike home. But to defend the Scottish revolution of 1306–29, and with it the independence of the Scottish kingdom, the Bruce Scots would have to dig in for another bloody slog of war across their own lands.

2

HALIDON HILL TO CHÂTEAU GAILLARD, 1332–35

'Thus was the kinrik of Scotlande
Sa hail in Inglis mennys hande
That nane durst thaim with say,
At sa gret myscheif war thai,
Bot childyr, that na kyndly skill
Had to deyme betwix gud and ill,
Na couythe noucht dreide thar wil to say,
For that kynge was a childe as thai.'
      Original Chronicle of Andrew of Wyntoun, *c*.1400-20.

For the children of Robert I's generation, brought up on war against England and the disinherited, the conflict of the 1330s was naturally to be identified as a patriotic cause and a question of birth-right. Yet it cannot be denied that the Bruce party were sustained throughout the period 1332–41 by those noble houses best rewarded by the old king and which thus had most to lose: others in their shadow would also use the war to build their own territorial empires and image as hammers of the English. Thus it was not simply the case, as the poet above suggests, that only children dared utter King David's name by late 1332.

With Mar's death, the Bruce guardianship seems to have been shared briefly by two senior figures: in the south, by the not-always loyal Patrick Dunbar, Earl of March, who was now wed to the sister of the late Guardian Randolph; and in the north by Sir Andrew Murray of Bothwell and Garioch, husband of David II's aunt, Christian, and son of Wallace's comrade in 1297. But when at the close of 1332 Murray was captured by Balliol's men, Sir Archibald Douglas, brother of the good Sir James, emerged to lead the fight. Joined by the teenage knights John Randolph, Earl of Moray, Robert Steward and William Douglas of Lothian, the Guardian scored an immediate victory on 17 December at Annan in Dumfriesshire. 'King Edward' was forced to take flight in the night half-dressed to Carlisle leaving his only brother, Henry Balliol, for dead as he fell alongside Walter Comyn of Kilbride and Sir John Mowbray. With its figurehead temporarily deserted the fragility of the Balliol coup was exposed. The burgh of Perth fell to the Bruce Scots once more: here Duncan, Earl of Fife, and his daughter and heiress, Isabella, were captured and sent to custody in Kildrummy Castle in Mar under Christian Bruce.

However, much like the Scots under Wallace after Stirling Bridge, the Bruce Scots must now have steeled themselves for an impending storm. For Balliol had withdrawn into the waiting arms in armour of Edward III. By now the English king had established his government at York, just like his grandfather, and persuaded his subjects to fund a war against Scotland to protect their own realm. By the beginning of the new campaign season at the end of March 1333, Balliol and an English force had reached Berwick where they besieged Sir Alexander Seton and Patrick, Earl of March, guarding this symbolic and strategic town and castle: Edward III and an army joined them in May. This time, though, the defenders certainly put up a far stouter show than the Balliol-Comyn regime of 1296. The English king was obliged to gamble Berwick's surrender against a deadline for the Bruce troops' relief by their comrades. But even when this date slipped past and Edward hanged Sir Alexander Seton's son, Thomas, in full view of Berwick's walls, the Scots held on. A substantial Bruce force was coming to their aid.

Yet when on 19 July this army engaged the forces of Edward III and Balliol at Halidon Hill the Bruce Scots gave the English king and his puppet exactly what they wanted: the chance to decide Scotland's fate in pitched battle. The resulting destruction of the Scottish ranks, allegedly at the cost of a mere handful of Anglo-Balliol casualties, was terrifying. Earls Hugh of Ross, Kenneth of Sutherland, Alexander Bruce of Carrick (rescued at Annan), John Campbell, Earl of Atholl, and Malcolm, Earl of Lennox, fell alongside Guardian Douglas, Sir Andrew Fraser and several of his kin as well as perhaps many Stewarts and other lesser knights: up to 100 Scots prisoners may have been beheaded after the battle on the orders of the English king. Looking on, Edward Balliol might easily have worried that this was no way to win the hearts and minds of his would-be subjects: this was turning into another vindictive English conquest, revenge for 1314 and 1327–8.

That this was so was made plain in February 1334 at a Balliol parliament at Holyrood Abbey (scene of the peace treaty closure in 1328). Here the vassal king of Scots repeated his alienation of much of Scotland's southern shires to Edward III and his heirs (although it should be noted that on this occasion he only agreed vaguely to grant 2,000 librates worth of land, still to be inspected and selected). In reality this merely confirmed on paper the English occupation of this region with its own garrisons and administrative regime since the previous summer's victory and the immediate surrender thereafter of Berwick: Earl Patrick of March's defection to the Anglo-Balliol camp at this time to protect his border lands was matched by many lesser southern Scots.

For their part, Balliol and the disinherited turned to dismantle the Bruce resettlement and to reclaim their lands in the north. But now strong signs also emerged that even within his own camp the personal monarchy of the fifty-year-old Balliol was a sham, a pretext for the territorial aggrandisement or restoration of other, younger, ambitious individuals. Not only did Edward III look to men like Malise, Earl of Strathearn, Gilbert Umphraville, Earl of Angus, and Sir Henry Beaumont (claimant of Buchan) to be his regional lieutenants in the north overseeing garrisons at Perth, Dundee and Stirling; but the English king also stepped in to determine the *status quo* of lordship in that 'pale' or war-zone. Recovering the persons of Duncan, Earl of Fife, and his heiress,

Isabella, Edward put the veteran earl back to work at Perth and shipped the girl off as his cousin to wardship in Northumberland: by controlling her marriage, Edward might determine the fate and loyalty of Scotland's premier earldom (just as Robert I had sought to do in 1315). Edward III also concluded a secret alliance with John MacDonald of Islay, the Bruces' former valuable ally in the west and now self-proclaimed 'Lord of the Isles'.

However, it was in the person of the charismatic and forceful David Strathbogie, Earl of Atholl and Lord of Strathbogie, that Edward III arguably found his best agent among the disinherited. This was a knight determined to restore his family's lordship north of the Forth and well able to rally the support of native men in that area through his marriage to the daughter of Henry Beaumont, claimant to the Comyn earldom: the painful memory of the Bruce herschip of Buchan must have brought many northern men to this camp's standard. In addition, Strathbogie also had claims to Fife and – at a push – the Scottish throne itself: with Balliol unwed and childless in late middle age, the young earl was thus perhaps viewed as the English Crown's best chance of policing their northern border in the years to come.

Strathbogie's importance was clearly recognised in early 1334 when he was appointed a regional lieutenant by Edward III and granted the vast Renfrew and Clydeside lands of Robert Steward, the heir presumptive to the Bruce throne. Indeed, it was Strathbogie's initial success in overrunning these lands which seems to have forced the Bruce party to finally take the decision to evacuate their child-king. David, his queen and sisters, the children of several noble families and a number of churchmen had taken shelter since 1333 in Dumbarton Castle in the care of the king's 'foster-father', Sir Malcolm Fleming of Biggar. But in May 1334 word was received from France – where John Randolph, Earl of Moray, had gone to activate the 1326 alliance – that the new Valois king, Philip VI, was willing to offer the Scots king refuge in his hour of need. Robert Steward, now seventeen and already blooded at the battle of Halidon Hill, had barely escaped by boat from his west coast lands with his charters and life to join his royal uncle in Dumbarton. But when David and his entourage set sail 'north-about' to France, the heir to the throne did not go with them as might have been expected. Instead, the Steward remained, punching a way out via the Clyde estuary for the king's boats in the face of Macdougall and English naval activity. A Bruce king was once more fleeing to escape destruction by his Scottish and English enemies. But thereafter, the Steward turned to the support of his west coast allies like the Campbells of Lochawe to recover his familial heritage, serving as guardian or 'king's lieutenant' in the west while John Randolph, Earl of Moray, acted in this capacity in the north and east.

Robert Steward's early success was impressive. Deploying galleys and Gaelic 'galloglass' troops like those used by the Bruces in Ireland, he recovered Rothesay and Bute killing the Balliol sheriff there, Alan Lyle, and pressed on inland. Linking up with the men of Renfrew and Lanarkshire, as well as of Annandale, Carrick, Cunningham and Kyle Stewart – many of them Bruce and Randolph tenants – he swept into the hotbed of the civil war, the south-west. According to at least one later Scottish chronicler, the Steward at this time 'began to attract certain brave men to his side, and to draw Scots of good sense towards him, to enlarge his army every day, and to attach their hearts to himself in mutual affection and firm loyalty. For he was then beginning to grow into a young man of attractive appearance above the sons of men, broad and tall in physique, kind to everyone, and modest, generous, cheerful and honest'. Much of this region now began to submit to him in David's name.

The Steward was, though, undoubtedly aided in his campaign by the distraction of the tensions and lack of leadership which had begun to emerge in the Balliol camp. By the autumn of 1334 Balliol had fallen out at his Perth HQ with Strathbogie, Beaumont and others over the fate of the varied southern and central Scottish lands of the Mowbrays. Unable to come to terms, Edward left for Berwick while Sir Alexander Mowbray defected, helping Sir Andrew Murray (now released) force Beaumont into yielding the Comyn castle of Dundarg in Aberdeenshire. Without the help of his father-in-law, Strathbogie was in turn vulnerable to attack: John Randolph, Earl of Moray, hunted him down in Lochaber in September 1334 and forced him to defect, tempting him into service as a Bruce lieutenant by offering him the recovery of his lands. All this meant that by the close of the year the Bruce Scots – down to their last four besieged castles in spring (Dumbarton,

27. Caerlaverock Castle, Dumfriesshire.
The Maxwells of Caerlaverock, suspected of colluding with Balliol in 1320,
would come out in support of the invasion of 1332: this formidable castle
was a key border strongpoint for both sides and had been besieged by
Edward I in 1300.

Lochleven, Kildrummy and Urquhart) – had recovered much of Scotland north of the Tay.

Nevertheless, internal tensions also bubbled to the surface in the Bruce camp about this time. Installed in dreary exile in Château Gaillard in Normandy and supplied with welcome French gold and victuals, David II's close councillors had apparently been alarmed by the progress of the Steward – the heir to the throne – in occupying Bruce and Randolph lands in south-west Scotland and in advancing his lordship into those titles left open by the power vacuum of the costly battles of 1332–3. The available evidence suggests, indeed, that by spring 1335 moves were afoot to have Steward replaced in the lieutenancy by Andrew Murray and Randolph. By the time of a Bruce war-council at Dairsie in Fife in April 1335 – held while the Scots were giving siege to Cupar Castle – factional lines had been drawn.

According to the Scottish chroniclers, at this meeting Strathbogie 'cleaved' to the side of the Steward and was opposed by Randolph, Murray, Alexander Mowbray, William Douglas of Lothian and the vacillating Earl of March. It is likely that Strathbogie – whom we are told had appeared with 'a great force' – had stoked Steward's fears for his inheritance and political position in the face of Bruce suspicion: Atholl may have offered him instead the chance to keep the lands his house had acquired by 1329 and perhaps to secure the earldom of Fife if he defected to Balliol and England. Those loyal to Gaillard, however, prevailed. By autumn 1335, Strathbogie was back in the English camp as Edward III's 'warden' in Scotland and the Steward arranged to defect. These two had undoubtedly been encouraged to do so by the presence of Edward III and Balliol at Perth in summer with a sizeable army which included a number of knights from the continent keen for sport: 'tarrying there until the arrival of the earl of Atholl, they plundered all the country around', cutting a swathe which caused much of the Lowland populace to take to the hills.

Thus by the end of this campaigning season it was the Bruce Scots who appeared back on the ropes. This was not least so because Randolph had been captured. According to Scottish sources he was taken in an ambush while chivalrously escorting a

28. Edward Balliol's seal
Crowned at Scone using his father's muniments in September 1332 in front
of many key Scots, Balliol nonetheless only held two or three parliaments
and was forced to grant much of southern Scotland to Edward III.

captive English ally, the Count of Gueldres, south for release; English chroniclers, by contrast, assert he was captured assaulting Roxburgh. Either way, Sir Andrew Murray was left alone to emulate his father and lead the fight from his hideaway in the forests of Perthshire.

3

MURRAY'S WAR FOR SCOTLAND, 1335–38

'...the great tyranny and cruelty this Earl of Atholl practised among the people words cannot bring within the mind's grasp: some he disinherited, others he murdered; and, in the end, he cast in his mind how he might wipe all the freeholders from off the face of the earth'.

Chronicle of John of Fordun, c.1380.

The autumn of 1335 would see some of the most bitter fighting between Scots since Robert I's attack on the Comyns in the north-east in 1307–8. The catalyst to this intense regional and in many ways personal combat was David Strathbogie's siege of Kildrummy Castle, then held by Sir Andrew Murray's wife, Christian Bruce of Garioch. Capture of this formidable stronghold, with its round-towers modelled on Edward I's Welsh castles, would bring control of the passes from Mar and Garioch through to the earldom of Moray, where Strathbogie already held Lochindorb Castle, and to the lordship of Strathbogie itself: Kildrummy also influenced access

to the hinterland of the vital sea-port burgh of Aberdeen and on north to Buchan and Banffshire.

So intensely did Murray feel the need to aid his wife that he secured English permission to break a short Anglo-Scottish truce then in force: that he was given leave to do was in part a reflection of just to what degree the English viewed Balliol's cause north of Forth as a purely Scottish affair. But as well as Patrick, Earl of March, and William Douglas of Lothian and their south-eastern followings, Murray was able to call upon the military support of many northern lords alarmed by Strathbogie's marauding and keen to smash their resurgent local rivals: the new Earls of Ross and Sutherland as well as perhaps the Keiths and Frasers and many of their neighbours had thus probably joined Murray before he outflanked and encountered Atholl's force in the forest of Culblean on 30 November 1335. 'Raging like bears or lions robbed of their cubs', Murray's men slaughtered their enemies in hand-to-hand combat with little quarter. The Earl of Atholl himself perished with his back to a tree.

A number of Atholl's following now resubmitted to the Bruce cause, including the Menzies of Fortingall: Murray then marched south to attempt once more to take Cupar Castle in Fife wherein 'were a great many Scots who had gone over to the English'. Bringing relatively secure control of the north-east and of Aberdeen, the battle of Culblean has thus been seen by many historians as a key turning point of the second phase of the Scottish wars. However, the threat of English military supremacy remained very real and Murray would not be able to really capitalise upon his destruction of Atholl until Edward III declared war on France in 1337 turning his energies to the continent and away from Scotland.

In 1336, though, the north-east paid a terrible price once more, this time for the death of Atholl. Edward III, Balliol and Beaumont, determined to save Atholl's wife who was besieged at Lochindorb, once more brought an army to Perth. After a small force had rescued the Countess, the Edwards set about 'consuming the whole of Moray with fire', sparing only the cathedral and priory at Elgin before burning and levelling Aberdeen. Edward III's

Opposite Page: 29. Sir Andrew Murray of Bothwell, King's Lieutenant 1335–8. Murray's destruction of David Strathbogie, Earl of Atholl, at Culblean in the north-east in November 1335 effectively ended the war effort of the disinherited Edward Balliol.

brother, John of Eltham, is said to have inflicted a similar herschip on west central Scotland, although accusations that churches there were fired with refugees trapped inside may be Scottish propaganda: the same might be true of Beaumont's alleged torture and execution of Bruce Scots from Culblean. But the English king only returned home after he had strengthened the defenses of Perth (at the expense of the clergy of Fife and Angus) and repaired and enlarged the garrisons at Dunnottar in the Mearns, Leuchars and St Andrews in Fife, and at the royal castles of Stirling, Edinburgh and Roxburgh. Like Edward I, he was clearly determined that the Scots should not threaten his control of the counties south of Forth as he geared up for war with France over the eternal issue of homage for Gascony.

In steadying themselves to harry this occupation network, the Bruce party was aided by its French ally's insistence that the Scots be included in all short truces with England negotiated either by Philip VI or by papal cardinals determined to bring Europe to peace so as to allow a crusade to the Holy Land, planned since the 1320s, to go ahead under the Valois king. It was this neutral third party interest which must have come up with the bizarre proposal in autumn 1336 that peace should be secured between England and Scotland by persuading David II to abdicate and to end his adolescent (and presumably unconsummated) marriage to Edward III's sister, Joan: this fifteen-year-old girl should then wed Edward Balliol (by then fifty-three) who would become king of Scots as the English Crown's vassal while David was compensated with land in England. It clearly did not take Murray long to relay his party's concurrence with Gaillard's scornful rejection of these terms. For by October 1336 Murray's army had emerged from the woods to level Dunnottar and the nearby minor castles at Kinneff and Lauriston.

The Scots then spent winter sheltering in the Angus woodlands before emerging early in 1337 to continue their erosion of Anglo-Balliol control. This was a war of attrition which inflicted long-lasting damage on these Lowland shires: in the words of Fordun's source, 'through the ceaseless marauding of both sides, the whole land of Gowrie, Angus and Mearns was, for the most part, almost reduced to a hopeless wilderness, and to utter want'. But by early spring, Murray – aided by the Earls of March and Fife and Douglas of Lothian – penetrated into Fife 'where he levelled with the ground the [Fife earl's own] tower of Falkland, plundered the land everywhere around, took the inhabitants prisoners, and put them up for ransom'. A three-week siege then reduced Leuchars and St Andrews Castle (where the bishopric had remained vacant since the death of Bishop Ben in 1333). Murray's next prize was his own Lanarkshire castle at Bothwell in March 1337.

However, when Murray then laid siege to Stirling Castle in April his military limits were reached. In the face of Edward III's final personal expedition north, once more to Perth, in summer 1337, Murray's forces withdrew to higher ground and declined battle. They were not really able to help Earl Patrick of March's wife, 'Black Agnes' Randolph, as she defied the English troops and king besieging Dunbar Castle. Yet this was to be the Bruce Scots' last major retreat. England's cold war with Philip VI finally turned hot that summer as Edward assumed the title of king of France. To this warrior English monarch, Edward Balliol had already long-since become a lost cause; now the Scottish campaign became a mere holding operation once more sorely under-resourced. Even knights like Beaumont and his English disinherited friends would prefer paid service on the continent, for which cause they abandoned their siege of Dunbar in July 1337.

Thus there followed a year of steady ground-swell for the Bruce Scots. Perth, Stirling and Edinburgh were all besieged. Although efforts to take the latter castle had to be abandoned because of 'the falsehood and deceit of certain Scotsmen' much of the Forth valley submitted to Murray in David's name: 'thereupon followed, on the part of both English and Scots, the wholesale destruction of Lothian'. But respite was to be had in a number of short Anglo-Franco-Scottish truces while French supplies arrived regularly through Dumbarton, a link exploited actively by clerics and knights relaying to David's court at Gaillard: the vital role played by this contact is underlined by the English capture of two Scottish ships returning from France about 1336-7 bearing 30,000 lbs of silver, arms, Scottish noblewomen and children and the Bishop of Glasgow who died defending 'charters, conventions and indentures which had been concluded between the King of France and the Scots'.

Murray's lieutenancy was thus a violent passage for the Scottish realm. As Fordun's source put it:

30. Kildrummy Castle, Mar.
This vital north-eastern stronghold, guarding routes north to Moray, was the
focus of fighting on a number of occasions throughout the Scottish wars, not
least when Andrew Murray mustered to prevent the Strathbogie Earl of Atholl
from capturing it from Murray's wife, Christian Bruce, in 1335.

'all the country he marched through, in his wars, he
reduced to such desolation and distress, that more
perished afterwards through starvation and want, than
the sword devoured in time of war'.

But under Murray's continued leadership, the Bruce Scots would
surely have gone on to wind back the Anglo-Balliol presence in
southern Scotland allowing their teenage-king to return home in
some style: in late 1337 or early 1338 Murray may even have
'wreaked great havoc in the county of Carlisle'.

But in the spring of 1338, Murray died in his northern castle of
Avoch, possibly from wounds sustained in battle. He would later be
interred in a hero's grave beside his former king and brother-in-
law, Robert I, at Dunfermline. But his untimely death left another
power vacuum in the Bruce leadership in Scotland. The man who
filled this gap would cause the inner tensions of 1335 to re-erupt,
complications which would set the Scots' cause down another
political path of infighting which would almost lead to disaster.

4

ROBERT STEWARD'S LIEUTENANCY, 1338-41

'Sir John de Stirling, warden of Edinburgh castle, was captured by craft by Sir William de Douglas... William summoned the castle to surrender, promising faithfully if those within would do so that both Sir John... and all those within the castle, should preserve life and limb and all their goods... but that if they refused to do so, he declared that he would cause Sir John to be drawn there at the tails of horses, and afterwards to be hanged on gallows before the gate, and all those who were prisoners there with him to be beheaded before their eyes'.

Chronicle of Lanercost, c.1346

From his own point of view, Robert Steward's resumption of the lieutenancy in 1338 was timely. Now twenty-two and the father of at least two sons there was no other obvious Scottish noble close to the Bruce dynasty able to take up this role: Randolph was still an English prisoner and David II was only fourteen and not likely to assume full power for a couple of years. But as lieutenant, Robert could also use his authority to extend his influence into the valuable earldoms of central Scotland now that Atholl was dead, Fife (born *c*.1283) was ageing and without a son and Malise of Strathearn had lost his Balliol patron. Moreover, after July 1338 Edward III would be committed fully to his campaign in France and unable to strengthen his Scottish border. Thus the Steward took up Andrew Murray's baton just as the tide turned and much of the hard work was done.

There remained, of course, much ground and many strategic sites for the Bruce Scots to recover. But increasingly over the next two years, this campaign was the focus not only of further local struggles to overturn the Anglo-Balliol occupation but of a growing contest between the Steward and David and his close advisors for control of policy and resources.

Those in Gaillard were perhaps right to be suspicious of the Steward's behaviour. Once more he is described in sympathetic Scottish sources as an extremely popular leader, one who:

> 'travelled through each province, accepting everyone who had adhered to the English to be loyal to king David and scrutinized everywhere the customs and deeds of his compatriots; and to prevent the poor from suffering malicious prosecution by the powerful, he diligently made enquiries to curb them. Then the kingdom began to prosper, the farmers to cultivate the fields, the church of God to be respected, monks to resume His service and to be restored to their former state...'.

In contrast, Scottish chroniclers favourable to David II and the Bruce regime saw only the Steward's self-interest and claimed that he 'was then not governed by much wisdom': this was the kind of vitriolic propaganda previously reserved for Balliol.

There does survive strong proof, though, that the Steward did seek to expand his political and territorial power before the return of his uncle, the king. In October 1339, at a parliament at Scone an assize was held which found Malise, Earl of Strathearn, innocent of treason and the charge of resigning his earldom to Edward Balliol. The Crown's re-opening of this case in 1344 makes it clear this is not the result the Bruce government sought against one of their former opponents. But it was perhaps a verdict which the Steward and others needed to use to protect themselves from charges of defection to Balliol: it may also have allowed the Steward to encroach on Strathearn, a title he would secure by 1357. But at the same time, the Steward also interfered in the collection of royal revenues in the north-east of Scotland reserved for dispatch to Gaillard through Aberdeen. Finally, when William Douglas of Lothian returned from a visit to David's court in Normandy in 1339 with several French knights and ships in tow to aid in the siege of Perth, the Steward sent these men home, apparently eager to oversee the assault himself. During the course of this campaign he is also reported to have clashed with William, Earl of Ross, justiciar (and perhaps with the powers of lieutenant) in the north who had been collecting revenues in Perthshire, the focus of Steward interests.

However, it should not be forgotten that, as in 1334–5, the Steward's three-year lieutenancy was also marked by significant gains for the Bruce party against the English and the disinherited. Perth fell in August 1339, its defenders reportedly reduced to cannibalism. This had been preceded by the surrender of Cupar Castle in Fife where Edward Balliol's chamberlain, a William Bullock – a man much respected by all sides and 'lieutenant and treasurer of all the English and their adherents in the kingdom of Scotland' – defected to the service of William Douglas of Lothian.

However, all of this was mirrored in France by David II's flexing of his military and political muscles. In 1339–40, the sixteen-year-old Scottish king is reported to have taken to the field under his own banners in the army of Philip VI against Edward III and his continental allies at Buironfesse in Flanders in a campaign which turned out to be an abortive stand-off. Nonetheless suitably impressed with the chivalry of war David must also have participated in some tournaments. He had grown into just the kind of young monarch who would be worried about the activities and mounting experience, following and progeny of his heir presumptive, the Steward.

Thus David's reasons for returning to Scotland in mid-1341 may have been dominated by political considerations within the Bruce party. The king may have become further concerned about his ability to assert royal authority after Douglas of Lothian and

Bullock captured Edinburgh Castle on 17 April, slipping a hay cart under the port-cullis and storming the castle in a surprise attack (rather than threatening the garrison as English chroniclers, quoted above, claimed). Stirling Castle was at that time also under intensive siege by the Steward and his divisions led by Ross and Sir Maurice Murray of Drumsargard (the castle finally fell in April 1342): at this rate there would be nothing significant left for David to lead his men to recover so as to mark his apprenticeship as his father's son. Extra pressure for David to leave Gaillard may also have come from the French, tired of paying his expenses and anxious that he should step up the Scottish war effort against Edward III. Both allies may have been energised by the news that in early 1341 Edward had been forced to return to Westminster in haste to deal with a political crisis provoked by an English parliament sick of war taxes and bad results.

All of these were compelling reasons for David to return to Scotland. But it is noticeable that these motives took little or no account at all of Edward Balliol. By 1341 that was perhaps a realistic reflection of the pretender's plight. Dropped by his English patron after 1338, Balliol had been reduced to skulking along the edges of the English administrative pale in southern Scotland. He was most often to be found at his manor house on Hestan Island in the Solway firth, the southernmost edge of his Galloway lordship. Several of the prominent south-western kindreds who had supported him after 1332 had now begun to drift into the Bruce party's peace, including the Macdowells and Maxwells: David would confirm a number of further Galloway chiefs in their lands in 1342–3. These defectors were also joined by a number of south-eastern and central Scottish lords anxious to preserve their lands, for example the Bissets of Upsetlington (Berwickshire), Tweedies of Drumelzier (Peeblesshire), the Ramsays (Fife, Lothian and Angus) and Murrays of Tullibardine (Perthshire). Aged fifty-eight, divorced and childless, Balliol was not likely to be a real threat ever again unless it suited his English masters.

5

The Uncertain Road to Neville's Cross, 1341–46

'[The French knights in Scotland] saw a poor country full of woods and mist. They joked about it, laughed amongst themselves and said "No wealthy man can be lord of a country like this".'

Chroniques of Jean Froissart, *c.*1385.

The first five years of David II's active adult rule were to be dominated by internal tensions rather than war with England and the disinherited. Nonetheless, much of this political in-fighting sprang from the fall-out from the violent Balliol disruption of Robert I's land resettlement. After scores of nobles had been killed, and many others forced or glad to defect since 1332, David had to oversee a further redistribution of key provincial titles and lesser baronies as well as Crown offices in order to assert his personal and dynastic authority over his subjects. He would find this especially difficult in certain quarters because the Steward, the Earls of March and Ross and knights like Douglas of Lothian – nobles who could claim to have been the patriotic defenders of the realm in the 1330s

31. The Battle of Neville's Cross, 1346.
The capture of David II by a minor English esquire and the defeat of his Scottish host owed much to the desertion of some of the king's disgruntled subjects (not the presence of Edward Balliol in the English force).

and thus self-made men – were prepared to challenge the king. They viewed him as a disruptive trespasser on their interests and really no better than their equal: as yet, they had no fear of David as Scots had had of his father.

David certainly made an inauspicious start, landing in June 1341 in near shipwreck at the small coastal toun of Inverbervie just north of Dundee rather than at Edinburgh or Dumbarton (which was controlled by the Steward). But thereafter the king set to work with a will, displaying considerable energy in touring much of the realm north of Forth and beginning to make significant grants of territory and offices so as to win support and check the influence of those he perceived as having grown over-mighty. By the close of 1341 his important grants had included the elevation of Malcolm Fleming as Earl of Wigtown, a first step to rebuilding

Bruce control of the sensitive south-west after the death of Alexander Bruce of Carrick (1333). William Douglas had in addition been made Earl of Atholl and lord of much of the middle and western border marches: this knight was also guardian of the massive southern inheritance of his teenage nephew, William, Lord of Douglas, nephew and heir of the 'good' Sir James. David himself had seemingly assumed control of Carrick and the former Bruce lordship of Annandale, despite John Randolph of Moray's ransom from captivity by 1342. Such largesse put the king well on the way to winning the loyalty of many men of chivalry.

Nor did David neglect warfare as a popular means of asserting his rule and binding his subjects' support. By February 1342 David would have participated in at least three raids across the border. However, it is fair to say that these were extremely tentative and lack-lustre affairs, often conducted under the banners of nobles rather than the king and steering well clear for now of English strongholds like Berwick or Edward Balliol's sympathisers in Galloway: these assaults were in no sense as ruthless and professional as the raids of Robert I and his lieutenants.

However, before David could really find his feet he found his powers questioned by the regional agendas of some of his great subjects, men anxious to protect and advance the influence they had fought to establish during the king's childhood exile. At a council in Aberdeen in February 1342 Douglas of Lothian and the Steward forced David to recognise their exchange of the former Strathbogie earldom of Atholl and the border lordship of Liddesdale, forfeited from Soules in 1320 and lost to the Bruces when Robert Bruce of Clackmannan (Robert I's illegitimate son) was killed in 1333. By thus sabotaging David's early attempts to redraw the map of lordship in Scotland to his advantage just as his father had done, the Steward's power in Perthshire was increased and Douglas became the dominant border lord.

So it was that when in summer 1342 Douglas 'of Liddesdale' seized and starved to death Sir Alexander Ramsay of Dalhousie, his chief rival in the borders, David was prevented from punishing him because Douglas was protected by the Steward. David had in part provoked this attack by granting Ramsay the sheriffdom of Roxburghshire after that knight had captured Roxburgh Castle in June 1342: this was an office and region Douglas viewed as his birth-right. But the king could do nothing to avenge the death of Ramsay, a royal favourite and the leader of a 'school' of chivalry in the Lothians, except lash out at one of Douglas's minor supporters, Bullock the Chamberlain: a vindictive David had him starved to death.

David was able to assume the patronage of Ramsay's Lothian followers. But the king was still painfully aware that as yet he did not have a sufficient military following of his own with which to challenge decisively such magnate power. Nor did he have ready resources to hand with which to rapidly build up such an affinity like his father. The destruction of the realm over the last decade had left much of the Lowlands as wasteland (as the comments of visiting French knights, quoted above, attest): even a key burgh like Edinburgh would return next-to-nothing to the Crown's coffers over the next five years. It would, then, be a slow, painstaking and piecemeal process for David to rebuild royal authority until it even approached a fraction of the stern and tight, hands-on control exercised by Robert I's regime – in the first flush of revolution – between 1309 and 1329.

But the second Bruce king did have time to do so. The preoccupation of Edward III in France – and a number of short truces to which the Scots were privy – meant that no English army would be seen in Scotland until the 1350s (other than a brief foray by Edward III to winter at Melrose in the winter of 1341–2). Thus David's careful use of patronage gradually began to have effect. He was unable (and probably reluctant) to punish those high profile Scots who had defected to English and Balliol service before 1341. Pardons and confirmations of all their lands were apparently granted to the Steward and Patrick, Earl of March. John MacDonald of the Isles was also able to protest in mid-1343 about David's interference in his west coast lands: although, in the end, the king had to give MacDonald's holdings in Kintyre to the Steward and the Isle of Skye to William, Earl of Ross. In June 1344 the king also had to defend in parliament at Scone his attempt to grant the key Perthshire earldom of Strathearn to another of the rising star knights of the 1330s, Sir Maurice Murray of Drumsargard. The Steward and Earl of Ross seemed intent on defending Malise, Earl of Strathearn, but a parliamentary assize of nobles – mostly favoured by the Crown – found him guilty of surrendering his earldom to the English and thus forfeit. With Maurice thus installed in these central lands, David's earlier restoration of John Logie (son of one of the Balliol conspirators of 1320) to the lordship of Strath Gartney in Menteith took on greater significance alongside the new earl of that region by marriage, Sir John Graham. This same 1344 parliament may also have enabled David to replace the Earl of Ross with John Randolph, Earl of Moray, as justiciar north of Forth. Finally, an attempt was made at Scone to impose peace upon the conflict raging in Lothian between the followers of Douglas of Liddesdale and the slain Alexander Ramsay: after his murder, the Scottish chroniclers assert,

> 'feuds and misunderstandings, undying, as it were, and endless, arose in the kingdom, not only among the lords, but even among the common people; so that, thenceforth, they murdered each other with mutual slaughter, and slew each other with the sword'.

By late 1344 to early 1345, then, David did seem to have the upper-hand over his greatest subjects. It was about this time that he may have expressed an interest in altering some of the parliamentary decisions taken by his father's regime about the royal succession. Clearly at odds with the Steward – who now had four sons – David wanted someone he could trust or control as his heir presumptive until such time as he had sons of his own. Siring his own heirs, however, was by no means a certainty as David's relations with his English queen may have been extremely troubled, perhaps aggravated by the war. Thus David turned to his sister Margaret Bruce and her husband William, Earl of Sutherland, married about 1342, to produce sons who would be *full* nephews of the king (out of the same mother's line): the Steward was only a *half*-nephew.

In this context, Robert Steward must have become increasingly paranoid about his political and dynastic position. As yet unmarried to the mother of his children he may have been holding out in hope of marrying Isabella, heiress to Fife. The Steward's panic in 1344 when a pretender Alexander Bruce, Earl of Carrick (the bastard of Edward Bruce, heir presumptive by an act of 1315), appeared in Scotland is thus understandable: but the Steward and Malcolm Fleming, Earl of Wigtown, seem to have put sufficient pressure on the king as to have this strange claimant executed. Nonetheless, when Earl William of Sutherland and Margaret

32. Hestan Island, Solway Firth.
After Edward III invaded France in 1338, Balliol was pushed out of south-west Scotland by the Bruce Scots and reduced to this lonely island fortress, gazing across the water at his birth-right.

Bruce produced a son called John in early 1346 the Steward must have wondered if his family's status and chance for the throne were slipping away: the Bruce regime had changed the succession before to suit its own ends, it might now do so again.

These uncertainties and tensions formed the backdrop to the military events of 1346. Edward III had prepared for an extended and intense campaign in France that summer. Forewarned, Philip VI had written to David and some of his nobles to persuade them to launch a diversionary attack on northern England. In spring 1346 the Scots may indeed have made a raid to *reconnoitre* across the west march as far as Penrith: but the mounting internal antipathies of the Scottish community may have diluted its impact with its leaders John Randolph and William Douglas reportedly bickering about their objectives. But by June 1346 Philip was desperate:

> 'I beg you, I implore you with all the force I can, to remember the bonds of blood and friendship between us. Do for me what I would willingly do for you in such a crisis, and do it as quickly and thoroughly as with God's help you are able'.

By August the French king would have his back to the wall, pinned down by Edward III's army a few miles from Paris. Again he wrote to David, this time advising him that the north of England – with all Edward's best fighting men in France – was as a 'defenceless void'.

David could not afford to put off repaying his debt to the French any longer. Yet in reality he was surely fully aware that there was little a Scottish invasion could do to halt the English advance on Paris. Indeed, David's final preparation of his royal host for an attack came *after* the French had been defeated at Crécy on 26 August. Thus in truth – just as with Edward II in invading Scotland in 1310 – David's summons of a Scottish army to enter England in late September 1346 was motivated more by a need to exploit what he assumed would be an easy military victory as a means of further asserting his authority over his own subjects. By making a prolonged progress through the undefended northern English counties – extracting tribute, plundering, burning and perhaps even seizing a castle or key walled town – David might recapture some of the Bruce magic and momentum of the raids of 1311–22 or 1327: he would be confirmed as his subjects' leader in war eroding the pulling power of nobles like the Steward and Douglas. Thus it was that in late September 1346 David assembled an army from all quarters of his realm and prepared to advance through the English countryside in style resting at night in magnificent tents and pavilions and bearing the symbol of a cross of St Margaret as a talisman for his troops.

However, it was at this moment that the political wrangling of the last five years rebounded on the Bruce king. Even before the army had set off, William, Earl of Ross, one of the great regional nobles frozen out of favour by David since 1341 because of his self-serving activities in the 1330s, murdered his local rival, Reginald MacRuaridh of Garmoran – a man favoured by the Crown – and abandoned the muster of the host taking his troops with him. Worse was to come. The Scots advanced unmolested over the next two weeks to within a few miles of Durham: all seemed set fair for a Bruce triumph. But on 17 October they were surprised by an English civil militia led by the Archbishop of York, Sir Ralph Neville and a number of other border lords. Nonetheless, the Scottish army of about 12,000 men should have defeated this force of no more than 8,000 including many archers. Yet not only did David and his generals chose poor ground where they were quickly compromised by the 'straytness of the place', Neville's Cross; but when the first two Scottish divisions of the cream of Scotland's chivalry led by David and his closest supporters were overwhelmed, the third Scottish division – perhaps placed deliberately at the back with the lighter, poorer troops under the Steward and the Earl of March – faced about and ran. According to an English chronicler:

> 'if one [March] was worth little, the other [the Steward] was worth nothing… these two turning tail, fought with success, for with their battalion, without any hurt, they returned to Scotland and thus led off the dance, leaving David to caper as he wished'.

In abandoning David the Steward must have assumed at first that he was going home to be king. All the men David had rewarded well since 1341 stayed to fight beside their monarch. But the death-toll was terrible. Randolph, Murray of Strathearn, Robert Keith the Marischal, Hay the Constable, the Chancellor and Chamberlain and much of the chivalry of the Lothians and northern Lowlands fell: Graham of Menteith was executed later by Edward III. In the end, David was extremely fortunate to be wounded in the face by arrows and captured (although by a mere English esquire) alongside Fleming of Wigtown, Douglas of Liddesdale, the Earl of Sutherland, Duncan, Earl of Fife and many other knights.

This of course meant that the Steward could not be king straight away. Yet it still remained uncertain as to just what status Edward III would accord his greatest prisoner. Would he recognise 'David de Brus' as the legitimate authority of Scotland and negotiate with his subjects for his release? Or would he instead revive the old Scottish civil war and the alternative claim to the throne? Edward Balliol must have thought that there was a good chance of the latter. For he had fought on the English side with eighty of his men at Neville's Cross. For Balliol, David's betrayal by some of his key subjects (and the Steward and March had defected briefly in the 1330s), the loss of most of his supporters and then his imprisonment by January 1347 in the Tower of London – perhaps in the former rooms of John Balliol must have been a pleasing sight.

6

Time runs out for Balliol, 1347–56

'In the mean whyle that King Davy was prisoner, the
lordes of Scotland, by a litle and a litle, wan al that they
had lost at the bataille of Duresme [Neville's Cross];
and there was much envy among them who might be
hyest; for every one rulid in his owne cuntery…'

Sir Thomas Gray's Scalachronica, c.1355

The battle of Neville's Cross eradicated any lingering humiliation
the English must have felt about Bannockburn. As David was led
to the Tower through the streets of London on a black horse
English songs and poems were composed about the Scots' well-
deserved defeat. In such a heady atmosphere Balliol must have
thought God had granted him a second chance.

But almost immediately it became apparent that the military,
political and financial priorities of Edward III would override any
opportunity for Balliol to make a come-back in the Scottish civil
war. The irony was that for David to be of any real value to the
English king he had to be recognised for all practical purposes as

king of Scots – if not always accorded his title: in that sense Neville's Cross would be more influential in bringing about a permanent Anglo-Scottish peace than Bannockburn. Moreover, it would have to be Edward III's main concern in any negotiations with the Bruce Scots about their lord's release to secure a neutral Scotland or, better still, an active ally or source of men and money against France. Despite his victorious campaigns of 1346 the English king was badly in need of such resources if he was to be able to defend the French ground he had won. Bargaining with David and his subjects was the only way for Edward III to do this without the cost of another full-scale northern war. The young Bruce monarch was, besides, Edward's brother-in-law and a more likely prospect for amicable relations in the future than the sixty-three-year-old Balliol: even if that pretender could be planted on the Scottish throne as an English vassal without an expensive war he would soon be dead without an heir.

Thus while Edward III ordered that all Scottish prisoners be handed over to the English Crown before they could be ransomed, Edward Balliol was once more reduced to pursuing a private enterprise in the north. In 1347–8 he would hire troops from Percy and Neville and raid into south-west Scotland, penetrating as far as Ayr and Glasgow before retreating to the newly formed English pale in the southern shires of Scotland: this border regime was based once more at Berwick, Roxburgh, Lochmaben and Caerlaverock. Edward III was surely happy to countenance such activity as a means of pressurising the Scots into talks. But there was no outpouring of support for Balliol in Scotland: if there was to be an alternative king to David it was Robert Steward who had quickly been elected 'king's lieutenant' by the Scots.

Indeed, Anglo-Scottish relations over the next decade were to be dominated on the one hand by an internal Scottish power struggle between David and the Steward and on the other by a period of messy, intermittent border warfare. Negotiations for David's freedom did not begin in earnest until 1348–9: by that time the Steward had made full use of his position and the royal seals to secure a legitimisation of his marriage and children and advance his control of Strathearn, Menteith and Fife (where the

Steward was bailie by 1347 and Earl Duncan would die in 1353). But the Steward would also be aided by the controversial nature of the terms first proposed for David's release.

Edward III's opening offers may have been designed to frighten the Scots into compromise: his renewed demands for homage for Scotland were never likely to succeed. But by the time the terrifying Black Death of bubonic plague reached Scotland after sweeping through England from mainland Europe in 1348–9 (claiming a third of the population) it is clear that David had become desperate to secure both his liberty and a chance to have his revenge upon his heir presumptive and other Scots who had deserted him in 1346 and now profited by his absence.

Thus new proposals, that Edward III or one of his sons be recognised as the heir to David's throne in the event of his failure to produce children, undoubtedly originated with the Bruce king. David was by now quite impressed with the chivalrous court and confident political power of his brother-in-law and wife's nephews: he was therefore quite prepared to take this gamble and form a military alliance with England if it meant his release without a heavy ransom and the chance to cancel out most of his concessions by siring a son of his own in the near future (he was still only twenty-six): better still, the Stewarts would be reduced in power. If this deal also meant restoring the Scottish lands of some of the heirs of those English and Scottish lords disinherited by Robert I – the last Strathbogie, Beaumont, Percy, Ferrers and Wake – then David was willing to do so: by 1353–4 the captive king would already have forgiven the Macdougalls of Argyll and Lorn sending their chief, John, back to Scotland to wed his niece, Joan Bruce, and as a potential replacement for the murdered MacRuaridh of Garmoran, thus providing a useful check on the MacDonald 'Lord of the Isles'. But in addition, David may also have been prepared to consider the use of force to get his way. By 1352, English troops were poised to enter Scotland with David to act against Robert Steward. Douglas of Liddesdale was also prepared to go along with this plan if he could secure his border lands: so much for the Scottish patriotism of this 'flower of chivalry' who along with a number of David's knights secured their liberty by swearing never to bear arms against England again.

33. The treaty of Berwick, 1357.
After eleven years of captivity and several attempts to secure his release were blocked by his heir-presumptive, Robert Steward, King David (pictured here without the robes) was finally liberated in return for hostages and a huge ransom to Edward III (with robes).

Such was Edward III's interest in this peace plan that David was paroled to Scotland in late 1351 or early 1352 to persuade his subjects to accept. The aged Edward Balliol's suspicions and the hopelessness of his situation were now confirmed. He must have been tipped off by the obvious favour and grace which Edward had extended to his brother-in-law, inviting David (but not Balliol) to the inaugural tournament of the royal Order of the Garter and St George at Windsor in 1348. Although Balliol managed to secure written guarantees from the English king that his family claim to the Scottish throne would not be prejudiced by these talks with David it was clear that negotiations with the Bruce had more to offer Edward III and his sons. By October 1351 Balliol had become so desperate that he even seems to have contacted the new king of France, Jean II, with an offer to defect, remarkably directing Jean to approach the Scots with the alternative of Balliol's leadership. For a short period Balliol was thus struck off the English payroll as 'king of Scots': money and this title were now extended to David. However, with the Steward heir to the Bruce throne and other key Scottish nobles committed to war against England, Jean II's offer was ignored: Balliol was soon reluctantly back on the English books.

However, Balliol may have taken some cold comfort from what happened next. In a parliament at Scone in February 1352 David's succession and alliance plan for his release was rejected by a majority of the Scots led by the Steward as lieutenant. The possibility of the Scottish throne passing to an English king or prince was probably unpalatable enough after six decades of war. But the proposal to restore some of the disinherited to their Scottish lands posed an intolerable threat of grave disruption to the Bruce land resettlement of 1314–29 and the changes in lordship effected in the 1330s: this was too much for the Stewarts, Douglases (now headed by William, Lord of Douglas), Dunbars, Rosses and many other lords and churchmen to accept. Moreover, in dismissing these terms and consigning David back to the Tower of London the Scots may have invoked the spirit of the Declaration of Arbroath. According to one English chronicler:

'the Scots refused to have their King unless he entirely renounced the influence of the English, and similarly refused to submit themselves to them. And they warned him that they would neither ransom him nor allow him to be ransomed unless he pardoned them for all their acts and injuries that they had done, and all the offences that they had committed during the time of his captivity, and he should give them security for that, *or otherwise they threatened to choose another king to rule them'*.

In other words, to defend the Bruce and Scottish revolution of 1306–29 the Scots in parliament in 1352 may have fallen back upon a principle which Robert I's regime had had no intention they should grasp.

In the end it would require another revolution before David secured his release: the complete reversal of French military fortunes. He almost got out of gaol in August 1354. Talks were then well advanced for a straight-forward release package in return for 90,000 merks and twenty Scottish noble hostages. But the Steward, the Lord of Douglas (who in 1353 had killed Douglas of Liddesdale), the Earl of March and others had their heads turned at the eleventh hour by French gold. Jean II dispatched an expeditionary force to Scotland in 1355 with this money. Hosts and visitors soon fell out, however, with the French aghast at the Scottish style of guerrilla warfare. What military success the Scots did achieve in 1355 came through their own efforts: March, Douglas and Sir William Ramsay attacked Norham while Thomas Stewart, Earl of Angus (the Steward's chamberlain), with March again managed to take Berwick town. These lords might have wished they had not stirred. For in retaliation Edward III summoned a host which recovered Berwick and wasted all of Lothian in the so-called 'Burnt Candlemas' of early 1356.

In Steward-controlled Scotland, however, such a destructive English attack could easily have been associated with David II's questionable diplomacy. Nor did it stop the Scots from sending a contingent to support Jean II fight Edward III's son, the Black Prince, and his army at Poitiers in September 1356. In this battle, though, William, Lord of Douglas, William Ramsay and several other Scots were able to do nothing to prevent the French defeat and the capture of their king. The English in turn were exhausted and over-stretched by their efforts. This altered radically David Bruce's position. Now Edward III could afford to release his Scottish captive on reasonable terms in return for money and a quiet Scottish border while he used Jean II to similarly extract what he wanted from France. The Steward and his associates now had to give in to mounting pressure in both Scotland and England for final release talks.

With this, Edward Balliol knew he had really reached the end of the road. His resignation of his claim to the Scottish throne to Edward III at Roxburgh in November 1356, as described by Fordun's Scottish source, merits coverage in full:

> Edward Balliol came, like a roaring lion, to meet him [Edward III]; and scarce containing himself for wrath, he broke forth into these words, more bitter than death itself, and said: 'O king, and best of princes! who art, I know, the mightiest of all mortals in the world in these days – I wholly, simply, and absolutely yield unto thee my cause, and all right I have, or may have, to the throne of Scotland, so that thou avenge me of mine enemies, the Scottish nation, a race most false, who have always cast me aside, that I should not reign over them' And as evidence that he did so he held forth unto him [Edward III], as he spoke, the royal crown, and some earth and stones which he picked up off the ground with his own hand. 'All these', quoth he, 'I give unto thee as a token of investiture. Only act, manfully, and be strong; and conquer for thyself the kingdom which ought formerly to have been mine'. This, moreover, should be noticed in this matter: that he [Balliol] gave away nothing from himself, inasmuch as he had no right, from the very first; and if haply he had had any, he then resigned it into another's hands.

In some senses these words, if true, echoed the document of resignation which John Balliol had been forced to sign for

Edward I in 1298. But they spoke to the bitter frustration of that disappointed king's son in 1356, now himself an old man without a cause. With that, Edward Balliol retired to live out his days tending his few remaining Yorkshire lands and tenants, living off a pension from Edward III. He died sometime in early 1364, aged eighty.

CONCLUSION

WINNING THE PEACE –
AFTER 1357

"Schyr', said he, 'sa God me save
The kynryk yharn I nocht to have
Bot gyff if fall off rycht to me,
And gyff God will that it sa be
I sall als frely in all thing
Hald it as it afferis king,
Or as myn elderis forouth me
Held it in freyast reawté"

John Barbour's *The Bruce*, *c*.1371–5

With Edward Balliol's resignation an official end was brought to a civil war which had really been all but over bar the shouting after the battle of Culblean in 1335. In October 1357 Edward III and David II and their subjects would agree the treaty of Berwick and the Bruce king would be released in exchange for twenty Scottish noble hostages and the promise of a ransom of 100,000 merks over the next ten years during which a truce would prevail: the war with England was also brought to a close – for now.

Upon his return home, though, David would be concerned with a different kind of Scottish civil war: a low-key, cold war between the Crown and its chivalric supporters on the one hand and the Steward and other regional magnates on the other. At first David had to recognise the status quo of lordship which had become entrenched during his second period of prolonged absence: in 1357–8 the king thus confirmed the Steward as Earl of Strathearn, the Lord of Douglas as the first Douglas Earl and Patrick, Earl of March, as heir to the earldom of Moray. However, David's obsession with cancelling out his ransom and establishing closer relations with England would see him revisit his plans for the admission of an English prince to his succession ahead of the Stewarts on several occasions. This diplomatic agenda was allied to David's determination to reduce the influence of these great regional magnates and specifically to deny the Stewarts control of Fife and Mentieth, prevent the Douglas Earl from dominating the border and force the Earl of Ross to sign away his lands to a Crown favourite.

Not surprisingly, these policies provoked a recurrent backlash from the Steward, his sons and various nobles. In 1359 David was forced to abandon a secret deal with England and to seek an (abortive) alliance with France. In 1360 David's mistress was murdered by frustrated magnates. Then in 1363 a rebellion by the Stewarts and the Earls of Douglas and March was swiftly crushed by the Crown and its well patronised supporters. David used the mandate of his swift victory over the rebels to marry for the second time (after the death of Queen Joan in England in 1362) and to approach Edward III to revive their peace treaty of 1351–2. This time, however, it was a measure of just how defunct the Balliol cause was that the English king offered to compensate the remaining disinherited with cash and English lands rather than insist upon their restoration to Scotland. In the end, though, such a change of terms was irrelevant. The Steward was able to rouse strong opposition in parliament in March 1364 (by which time Edward Balliol was probably dead). David's plan was again denounced as a threat to the very integrity of the Scottish realm and its institutions of state, law, Church and trade: worse still for the king, the Steward and his camp were able to claim that David was betraying the sacrifice of so many Scots in his name since 1332 as well as dishonouring the cause of his father, Robert I, 'such a wise, vigorous and able man'.

It was this ability to adopt a patriotic political stance as heir presumptive to the throne – recognised by an acts of succession of 1318 and 1326 – that would enable Robert Steward, along with the Earl of Douglas and others, to ride out David's harassment of their influence in Scotland throughout the rest of the 1360s. The second Bruce king may indeed have been a wily politician who never gave up on his attempts to displace the Stewarts and sire his own heir (even planning to divorce and take a third wife): he undoubtedly had '*raddure*' or guts as the chroniclers put it. But at the end of the day he was never as convincing or intimidating a king as his father, unable simply to impose his will on his subjects: the magnate kindreds whom Robert I had elevated and delegated power to in his name had become too autonomous and self-conscious of their position during David's childhood exile and captivity. But it is surely likely that the second Bruce king would have had some trouble with this next generation of magnates even if he had assumed the throne early and remained in place. In some senses the culling of Dupplin and Halidon Hill in 1332–3 and the destruction there of many nobles had simply delayed the inevitable. By the late 1360s David was, though, once more surrounded by ambitious regional noble chiefs and scions. If he had not died prematurely, aged just forty-seven (perhaps from unhealed wounds sustained in 1346), he would surely have faced a civil war between competing magnate interests which he could never have been sure to win.

In February 1371, then, Robert Steward succeeded unexpectedly as King Robert II. Throughout his reign his authority would be severely diluted and twice directly removed by great regional magnates, including his own sons. Even before he was crowned, his right of succession was allegedly challenged by William, Earl of Douglas. However, by claiming to be eligible for the throne himself as a descendant of the Balliols or Comyns, Douglas gave voice to the last flicker of that Scottish civil war begun in 1286: he was not really serious and was soon bought off with concessions of near-regal power in the borders as chief March Warden facing the 'auld enemie'.

The desire to resume hostilities with the Plantagenets was what bound the Stewarts and Douglases at this time. These two kindreds were the most successful powers to emerge intact from the civil hostilities of *c.*1306–71, claiming nine earldoms and the lordships of Badenoch, Galloway and Liddesdale at least between them by 1380. With David II gone they could denounce the ambivalent pandering to England of the last twenty years and lay claim to be the real heirs of Robert Bruce, the hero king. Just as he had been so they were the realm's bastions against the English: their political power rested firmly and legitimately upon that image and fact.

It was in the course of wrapping themselves up in the flag of patriotism (or, in the Douglases' case, the red Bruce heraldic heart) that the Stewarts and Douglases paid for Archdeacon John Barbour of Aberdeen to pen his epic romantic poem, *The Bruce,* by 1375. However, this was not just a work of courtly chivalry and lion-rampant Anglophobia. It was also a propaganda refutation of David II's dealings with England and his undermining of the Stewart succession. But, most importantly of all, it was a final means of rewriting the history books and public consciousness by asserting the right of the Bruce cause over that of Balliol.

Thus in Barbour's version of events the questionable manoeuvring and successive swapping of sides of the Bruces before 1306 is whitewashed: there is no attack on Galloway by the Bruces in 1286; no 'process at Norham' where the Bruces submitted to Edward Longshanks first; no defection by the Earl of Carrick to the English in 1302. Instead, in *The Bruce,* Edward I offers Robert Bruce the kingship in 1286 as his vassal first of all but is turned down in the cause of the tradition of free Scottish royalty. King Edward then offers the vassal throne to John Balliol who accepts. Balliol, however, 'was king bot a litill quhile' and quickly stripped of office by his overlord: this is the only mention King John gets in over 13,000 lines of Barbour's poetry: nor is there any mention of William Walllace.

The cause of fighting the English according to Barbour fell instead on the sturdy shoulders of Scotland's two greatest sons, Bruce and the 'good' Sir James Douglas. Three-quarters of the poem follows the hardships and triumphs of these two, rightful king and perfect knight, up to Bannockburn, including Comyn of Badenoch's betrayal of Bruce in 1306. After 1314 the rest of the reign is covered quickly as a period of stability and success under 'Good King Robert': the Irish campaign fails because of the arrogance of Edward Bruce, not Robert; the Soules conspiracy is a flop (with Edward Balliol never mentioned) and King Robert gives Umphraville gracious leave to quit the kingdom (in fact he threw him in gaol). Barbour's history of the reign then concludes with the coronation of David Bruce in a parliament which also sees the Act of Succession recognising Robert Stewart as heir presumptive, the treaty with France and the peace with England (including David's marriage) completed all at once: everything is put safely to bed before Robert's Arthur-like demise and the pilgrimage of Douglas to the Holy Land with his heart.

This work became the favourite courtly reading of the Stewart kings and their great magnates and lesser subjects throughout the late fourteenth and fifteenth centuries. A similar version of events after the death of Alexander III also entered the Scottish chronicle tradition and popular historical memory. Things had very nearly gone awry for the Bruce cause in 1292 and 1306. But Robert I had clearly won the civil war: his chief supporters preserved his dynasty and the realm against a second English and Balliol attack after 1332. And because of the unusual diplomacy of his son, David, after his capture in battle in 1346, Robert Bruce became the national icon invoked by the generation of that other famous Scottish victory over England, the battle of Otterburn of 1388, and in subsequent attempts by Stewart kings of Scots over the next 150 years to recover Roxburgh and Berwick from Plantagenet control. John and Edward Balliol, the Comyns, the other disinherited lords and, in his own way, David II, were the early Scottish casualties of this long war.

A Guide to Further Reading

In a book of this nature it is impossible to provide an exhaustive bibliography for the wars but the following are suggestions for the most important and accessible works for anyone interested in this period.

The standard, groundbreaking text for the first phase of the Scottish wars remains G.W.S. Barrow's *Robert the Bruce and the community of the realm of Scotland* (3rd edn, 1988). Alternative views can be found in the following general works: R. Nicholson, *Scotland: the Later Middle Ages* (1974); A. Grant, *Independence and Nationhood: Scotland, 1306–1469* (1984).

For Anglo-Scottish relations and the kingdoms before 1286 the best single volume is A.A.M. Duncan, *Scotland: the Making of the Kingdom* (1975). Recent 'British history' approaches have been extremely rewarding – see R.R. Davies, *The First English Empire: Power and Identities in the British Isles, 1093–1343* (2000); R. Frame, *The Political Development of the British Isles, 1100–1400* (1995) or the more traditional W. Ferguson, *Scotland's Relations with England: a survey to 1707* (1979); K.J. Stringer's *Earl David of Huntingdon: A Study in Anglo-Scottish History* (1985) contains much about the pre-1286 history of the key families of the wars. For Scotland in the thirteenth century: A. Young's *Robert the Bruce's Rivals: the Comyns, 1212–1314* (1997) is extremely useful as is N. Reid ed., *Scotland in the Age of Alexander III* (1988) – a similar volume for the reign of Alexander II, edited by R. Oram, is forthcoming.

For the interregnum and 'Great Cause' much is to be found in the special edition of the *Scottish Historical Review* journal for 1990 which contains papers by G.W.S. Barrow, M. Prestwich, K. Helle and B. Crawford on the Maid's marriage talks. That journal's 1982 edition also contains N. Reid, 'The Kingless Kingdom: the Scottish Guardianships of 1286–1306'. Two further must-read articles are A.A.M. Duncan's 'The Process of Norham, 1291', in P.R. Coss and S.D. Lloyd eds, *Thirteenth Century England V* (1993) and G. Stell's 'The Balliol Family and the Great Cause of 1291–2' in K.J. Stringer ed., *Essays on the Medieval Nobility of Scotland* (1985): the latter is a volume which also contains a valuable paper by Barrow and A. Royan on 'James the Steward'. For the wars of 1296–1302 see A. Fisher, *William Wallace* (1985) and E.M. Barron, *The Scottish Wars of Independence* (1934, reprinted 2000). For the all-important English perspective see F. Watson's excellent *Under the Hammer: Edward I and Scotland, 1286–1307* (1998). M. Prestwich's *The Three Edwards: war and state in England, 1272–1377* (1980) is also essential as are the same author's many articles and his *Edward I* (1984). For the fluid state of border identity in this period see: A. King's 'Englishmen or Scots? Choosing Sides in the Anglo-Scottish Wars in Northumberland, 1296–1307', *Northern History* (2002). For the diplomacy of 1298–1302 see R.J. Goldstein, 'The Scottish Mission to Boniface VIII in 1301', *Scottish Historical Review* (1991) and A. Stevenson, 'The Flemish Dimension of the Auld Alliance' in G.G. Simpson ed., *Scotland and the Low Countries, 1124–1994* (1996). N.A.T. Macdougall's *An Antidote to the English: the Auld Alliance, 1295–1560* (2001) provides a long-term view of Scotland's French support.

For Bruce's war and reign after 1306 much recent work should be added to Barrow's seminal study: A.A.M. Duncan's *The Nation of the Scots and the Declaration of Arbroath* (1970) and 'The War of the Scots, 1306–23', *Transactions of the Royal Historical Society* (1992); C. Neville, 'The Political Allegiance of the earls of Strathearn during the Wars of Independence', *Scottish Historical Review* (1986); A. Ross, 'Men for all Seasons? The Strathbogie Earls of Atholl and the Wars of Independence', *Northern Scotland* (2000-1); N. Reid, 'Crown and Community under Robert I', in A. Grant and K.J. Stringer eds, *Medieval Scotland* (1993); G.G. Simpson, 'The Declaration of Arbroath revitalised', *Scottish Historical Review* (1977); R.D. Oram, 'Bruce, Balliol and the Lordship of Galloway', *Transactions of the Dumfriesshire and Galloway Natural History and Antiquarian Society* (1992); M. Penman, 'A fell coniuiracioun agayn Robert the douchty king: the Soules conspiracy of c.1318–20', *Innes Review* (1999); and R. Tanner, 'Cowing the Community? Coercion and Fabrication in Robert Bruce's Parliaments, 1309–18', in K. Brown and R. Tanner eds., *Parliament and Politics in Scotland: 1286–1567* (forthcoming). C. McNamee's brilliant *The Wars of the Bruces: Scotland, England and Ireland, 1306–28* (1997) should not be missed and many useful articles on the Irish campaign have recently been gathered together by Tempus in S. Duffy ed., *Robert the Bruce's Irish Wars* (2002). For a fresh take on the peace see S. Cameron and A. Ross, 'The Treaty of Edinburgh and the Disinherited (1328–1332)', *History* (April 1999). R.J. Goldstein's *The Matter of Scotland: a historical narrative in Medieval Scotland* (1993) is a splendid analysis of the war of propaganda for which J.E. Fraser 'A Swan from a Raven: William Wallace, Brucean Propaganda, and Gesta Annalia II', *Scottish Historical Review* (2002) should also be consulted.

For the wars after 1329 the best starting point remains: R. Nicholson, *Edward III and the Scots, 1327–35* (1965); but see also C. Brown, *The Second Scottish Wars of Independence* (2002). An interesting perspective can be found in B. Webster, 'Scotland without a King, 1329–41', again in Grant and Stringer eds, *Medieval Scotland* (1993). For David II's problems see: M. Penman, 'The Scots at the Battle of Neville's Cross, 17 October 1346', *Scottish Historical Review* (2001) and my forthcoming *The Bruce Dynasty in Scotland: David II, 1329–71*. The only available work on David's rival is: R.C. Reid, 'Edward Balliol', *Transactions of the Dumfriesshire and Galloway Natural History and Antiquarian Society* (1956-7). For the diplomacy of 1346–71 see A.A.M. Duncan, 'A Question about the Succession, 1364', *Scottish History Society* Miscellany xii (1994).

A number of chronicles from the period are also now readily accessible in translation. For Scotland see *John of Fordun's Chronicle of the Scottish Nation*, ed. F.

Skene (2 vol. reprint, 1997) and *Walter Bower's Scotichronicon*, eds D.E.R. Watt et al. (9 vols, 1987–99), vols v, vi and vii. For England see *The Chronicle of Lanercost* ed. H. Maxwell (2 vol. reprint, 2001) and Sir *Thomas Gray's Scalachronica*, ed. H. Maxwell (reprint, 1999). For France see *Jean Froissart's Chronicles*, ed. G. Brereton (1968). A.A.M. Duncan's edition of *John Barbour's The Bruce* (1997) has a marvellous introduction and notes.

There are also several valuable documentary collections (in which most of the quotations for this book were found) of which the easiest to use are: *E.L.G. Stones ed., Anglo-Scottish Relations, 1174–1328* (1970) and E. Carmichael, E. Hamilton and N. Shead eds, *Sources for the Study of the Scottish Wars of Independence 1249–1329* (Scottish CCC Highers 1998): C. Brown is also preparing a larger collection of material relating to Robert Bruce for publication by Tempus in 2003. Finally, P.G.B. McNeill and H.L. MacQueen eds, *Atlas of Scottish History to 1707* (1996) contains many useful maps and commentaries about the wars.

LIST OF ILLUSTRATIONS, MAPS AND DIAGRAMS

1. The Seal of Alexander III (1249-86). Author's collection.
2. Marjorie, heiress of the earldom of Carrick, 'kidnaps' and marries Robert Bruce. By Alfred Pearse from T. Thomson's *A History of the Scottish People* (1893).
3. Monument to Alexander III, Kinghorn, Fife [author's collection].
4. Seal of the Scottish Guardians, 1286-92. Richard Oram, *Kings and Queens of Scotland* (2001).
5. John Balliol, Edward I, Robert Bruce of Annandale and the Maid of Norway. After William Hole's nineteenth-century frieze in the Scottish National Portrait Gallery.
6. The ruins of Norham castle, Northumberland. Author's collection.
7. Seal of King John (1292-6). Richard Oram, *Kings and Queens of Scotland* (2001)
8. John's submission to Edward I, 1292-3. After an original manuscript in the British Library, London.
9. The Stone of Scone under the Westminster coronation chair. Author's collection.
10. Toom Tabard, 1296. Richard Oram, *Kings and Queens of Scotland* (2001).
11. William Wallace. After N.C. Wyeth in J. Porter's *The Scottish Chiefs* (1921).
12. Robert Bruce, earl of Carrick, and his second wife, Elizabeth de Burgh. Richard Oram, *Kings and Queens of Scotland* (2001).
13. The murder of John Comyn of Badenoch, February 1306, Dumfries. Richard Oram, *Kings and Queens of Scotland* (2001).
14. Inverlochy castle, Lochaber. Author's collection.
15. Robert I's seal. Richard Oram, *Kings and Queens of Scotland* (2001).
16. Galloglas warriors of west Scotland. After R.S. Rait, *The Making of the Nations – Scotland* (1911).
17. The battle of Bannockburn, 1314. After F.M.B. Blaickie in J. Lang's *The Story of Robert the Bruce* (1905).
18. Cambuskenneth abbey, Stirling. Author's collection.
19. Tomb of Angus Og MacDonald (d. 1318). Fiona Watson *Scotland: A History* (2000).
20. The face of a hero? After model by forensic artist, Richard Neave.
21. Braveheart Bruce? After a design by Victoria Oswald and Historic Scotland.
22. Sweetheart abbey, Kirkcudbrightshire. Author's collection.
23. Where do ex-kings go to die? Photo: Amanda Beam.
24. The death-bed letter of Robert I, 1329. Richard Oram, *Kings and Queens of Scotland* (2001).

25. The tomb of Sir James Douglas (d. 1330), St Bride's church, Douglas. Author's collection.
26. Edward Balliol, Andrew Murray, Archibald Douglas, Randolph and the boy king, David II. After William Hole's 19th century frieze in the Scottish National Portrait Gallery.
27. Caerlaverock castle, Dumfriesshire. Author's collection.
28. Edward Balliol's seal. Richard Oram, *Kings and Queens of Scotland* (2001).
29. Sir Andrew Murray of Bothwell, King's Lieutenant 1335-8. After W.H. Margetson in T. Thomson's *A History of the Scottish People* (1893).
30. Kildrummy castle, Mar. Author's collection.
31. The Battle of Neville's Cross, 1346. After an original manuscript in the Bibliothèque Nationale, Paris.
32. Hestan island, Solway firth. Richard Oram, *Kings and Queens of Scotland* (2001).
33. The treaty of Berwick, 1357. After an original manuscript in the British Library.

MAPS

1. Map of Scotland. Author's drawing.

GENEALOGY

1. The Royal Succession. Author's illustration.

INDEX

Aberdeen, 69, 86, 121, 127, 131

Acts of Succession, 82, 85, 133, 147, 149

Alexander I, King of Scots (d. 1124), 16, 18

Alexander II, King of Scots (d. 1249), 20, 23-4, 55, 88

Alexander III, King of Scots (d. 1286), 13, 15, 21-8, 29-32, 39, 55, 72, 88, 149, *17, 27*

Anglo-Scottish relations, 12-4, 15-28 [to 1286]

Angus, earls/earldom of, 26, 30, 46, 54, 81, 92, 98, 109, 122, 128

Annan, battle of (1332), 112, 114

Annandale, 11, 13, 23-4, 28, 32, 46, 51, 54, 115, 131

Arbroath Abbey, 82, 85, 92

Atholl, earldom of, 35-6, 41, 81, 117, 126, 131

Balliol, Edward (d. 1364), King of Scots, 14, 28, 34, 41, 43, 46, 54, 84-6, 88, 103, 105-18, 121-3, 126-8, 129-32, 136-7, 141, 143-6, 149, *110, 118, 134*

Balliol, family of, 12, 14, 22-4, 26, 147

Balliol, Henry (d. 1332), 28, 34, 41, 46, 112

Balliol, John (I), of Barnard Castle (d. 1268), 23-4, 27, *96*

Balliol, John (II) (d. 1314), King of Scots (1292-6), 11, 23-4, 26-7, 29, 34-8, 39-46 [reign], 51, 53 [release 1299], 55-6 [release 1301], 59, 61, 72, 78 [death], 136, 143, 148-9, *33, 40, 42, 45, 101*

Bannockburn, battle of (1314), 76-8, 79, 81, 83, 86, 137-8, 149, *77*

Barclay of Brechin, family of, 30, 56, 73, 78, 85-6

Beaumont, family of, 81, 98-9, 105, 108, 113-5, 121-3, 139

Bek, Bishop of Durham, 34, 36

Bernard de Linton, Abbot of Arbroath (d. 1331), 82, 106

Berwick, treaty of, 1357, 145, *140*

Berwick-upon-Tweed, 37-8, 46-7, 50, 73-4, 83, 85, 88, 98, 112, 115, 131, 138, 142, 149

Birgham, treaty of (1290), 35, 41

Boyds, family of, 64, 68, 81

Bruce, Alexander (d. 1307), 28, 64, 66-7

Bruce, Alexander, Earl of Carrick (d. 1333), 106, 109, 113, 131, 133

Bruce, Christian (d. 1357), 92, 112, 119

Bruce, Edward (d. 1318), 34, 64, 66, 68, 70-1, 74-8, 81-4, 106, 133, 149

Bruce, family of, 11-4, 17, 22-3, 26, 31, 46, 99

Bruce, Isabella, 34, 41, 66

Bruce, Margaret (d. 1346), 133-4

Bruce, Marjorie (d. 1317), 64, 66, 81-2

Bruce, (Mary and Maud), 64, 66, 92

Bruce, Neil (d. 1306), 64, 66

Bruce, Robert, of Annandale, the 'old Competitor' (d. 1295), 24, 26, 29, 32, 35-42, *33*

Bruce, Robert (d. 1304), 26, 40-1, 50-1, 56, 61, *25*

Bruce, Robert, Earl of Carrick, King of Scots (1306-29), 11-4, 28, 34, 41, 50-1 [in 1297], 52-4 [as Guardian c.1298], 55-8 [re-submits to Edward I], 60-1 [plans bid for throne]; 62-4 [murders Coymn, made King], 65-72 [war in Scotland to 1310], 73-8 [war 1310-4]; 79-82 [and patronage]; 83-5 [and Irish invasion]; 85-6 [crisis of 1318-20]; 87-9 [war, 1320-3]; 91-2 [peace talks, 1323]; 92-4 [domestic kingship 1323-7]; 95-7 [war, 1327]; 978-100 [peace talks 1328], 102-7 [last year and death, 1329], 109-11, 114, 119, 124, 129, 131-2, 139, 142, 147-9, *57, 70, 77, 90, 93, 102*

Bruce, Robert of Clackmannan and Liddesdale (d. 1332), 86, 109, 131

Bruce, The, by John Barbour, 29, 63, 29, 145, 148-9, *93*

Bruce, Thomas (d. 1307), 64, 66-7

Buchan, earldom of, 11, 24, 68 [herschip of 1308], 81, 98-9, 113, 121

Bullock, William (d. 1342), 127, 132

Caerlaverock Castle, 54, 73, 109, 138, *116*

Cambuskenneth Abbey, 61, 76, 78, *80*

Campbells of Lochawe/Earl of Atholl, 67, 81, 92, 113, 115

Carlisle, 18, 20, 26, 42, 46, 51, 56, 83, 89, 91, 124

Carrick, earldom of, 13, 28, 32, 46, 51, 56, 64, 66, 82, 100, 115, 131, *25*

Church, Scottish, 13, 17-8, 20, 28, 35-6, 71-2, 81, 88, 146

Comyn, Alexander, Earl of Buchan, Guardian of Scotland (d. 1289), 30, 32

Comyn, family of, 17, 21, 24-6, 28-38, 40,

44, 48, 53–4, 56, 73, 78, 108, 119, 147, 149
Comyn, John, Earl of Buchan (d. 1308), 11–2, 46, 54, 56, 62, 68–9
Comyn, John (II), Lord of Badenoch, Guardian of Scotland (d. 1303), 30, 32, 36
Comyn, John (III), Lord of Badenoch, Guardian of Scotland (d. 1306), 11–2, 52-6, 60, 62–4, 66, 149, *63*
Comyn, Walter of Kilbride (d. 1332), 108, 112
coronation, rite of, 18, 106–7, 149
Courtrai, battle of (1302), 60
Crécy, battle of (1346), 135
Cressingham, Hugh, 47–8, 50–1
crusades to Holy Land, 19, 26, 44, 72, 100, 106, 122, 149, *104*
Culblean, battle of (1335), 121–2, 145
Cupar Castle, 117, 121, 127

Dail Righ, battle of (1306), 66
David I, King of Scots (d. 1153), 16–8, 23
David II/Bruce, King of Scots (1329-71), 19, 92, 94, 98–9, 105–14 [minority in Scotland], 114–28 [exile in France], 129–36 [rule 1341-6], 137–44 [captivity in England], 145–7 [rule 1357-71], 149, *110, 120, 140*
David, Earl of Huntingdon (d. 1219), 23–4, 38
Declarations, 71–2 [of clergy, 1309], 72 [of nobility, 1309], 85, 87–8, 141 [of Arbroath, 1320]
Devorguilla, Countess of Galloway (d. 1290), 23, 26, 36, *96*
'Disinherited', the, 81, 86, 91, 97–9, 105–10, 123, 139, 141, 149
Douglas, Archibald, Guardian of Scotland (d. 1333), 112-3, *110*
Douglas, Sir James (d. 1330), 64, 66, 68, 74–5, 81, 83, 85–6, 92, 94, 97–8, 100, 103, 106, 112, 131, 148–9, *104*
Douglas, Sir William (d. 1299), 50, 64
Douglas, Sir William, of Lothian/Liddesdale (d. 1353), 92, 112, 117, 121–2, 125, 127–9, 131–2, 135–6, 139, 142
Douglas, William, Lord/Earl of Douglas, 131, 141–2, 146–7
Dumbarton Castle, 100, 114–5, 130
Dumfries, 31, 62–4, *63*
Dunbar battle of, 1296/Castle/earls/earldom, 24, 30–1, 46, 123
Dunbar, Patrick, Earl of March (d. 1368), 73, 75, 78, 85–6, 109, 112–3, 117, 121–3, 129, 132, 136, 142, 146
Dundee, 50, 73-4, 113, 130

Dunfermline burgh/abbey, 91–2, 100, 108, 124, *90*
Dupplin, battle of (1332), 109, 147
Durham, 23, 26, 75, 97, 106, 135

Edgar I, King of Scots (d. 1107), 16
Edinburgh/Edinburgh Castle, 31, 55, 73–4, 89, 97–8, 122–3, 125, 128, 130
Edinburgh-Northampton, treaty of (1328), 95, 98–9, 105
Edward I, King of England (1272–1307), 11, 14–5, 21–2, 26, 28, 32, 35–9, 41–4, 46–8, 51–3, 55–6, 59–67, 72, 99–100, 107, 119, 122, 144, 148, *33, 42*
Edward II, of Caernarvon, prince of Wales, King of England (1307–27), 34, 54, 67, 74–9, 83–6, 88–91, 95–9, 108, 135
Edward III, King of England (1327–77), 14, 96–9, 103, 107–10, 112–4, 117, 121–3, 126–8, 132, 134–6, 137–46, *140*
Elizabeth de burgh, Queen of Scotland (d. 1327), 64, 92, 99, *57*
Eric II, King of Norway, 22, 34–5, 41

Falaise, treaty of (1174), 19, 21
Falkirk, battle of (1298), 11, 52
Fife, earls/earldom/shire of, 17, 18, 22, 26, 28, 41, 81, 92, 107–9, 114–5, 122, 126, 128, 138–9
Fife, Duncan, Earl of, Guardian of Scotland (d. 1288), 30, 32
Fife, Duncan, Earl of (d. 1353), 64, 73, 78, 85, 92, 107–9, 112–4, 122, 136, 139
Fleming, Malcolm, of Biggar, Earl of Wigtown, 114, 130–1, 133, 136
Fochart, battle of (1318), 83–4
France/the French, 19, 20, 22, 32, 43–4, 51, 53–6, 60, 72, 78, 94, 96, 105–6, 114, 117, 121–3, 126–8, 129, 132, 134–5, 138, 141–2, 146, 149, *101*
Fraser, family of, 30, 60, 81, 109, 113, 121
Fraser, William, Bishop of St Andrews, Guardian of Scotland (d. 1297), 30, 32–6, 41, 43, 61

Gaillard, Château, 117, 122–3, 126–7
Galloglas/Gaelic troops, 66–70, 82–4, 115, *71*
Galloway, 13, 20, 22-3, 36, 41, 54, 67, 69, 71, 82, 92, 98, 100, 109, 128, 131, 148
Garioch, 24, 31, 36, 92, 119
Glen Trool, battle of (1307), 67
Gordon, Sir Adam, 62, 73, 78, 92
Graham, Sir David, 12–3
Graham, Sir John, Earl of Menteith (d. 1346), 133, 136
Great Cause, The (1291-2), 38, 41, 58

Halidon Hill, battle of (1333), 112–4, 147

Harcla, Andrew (d. 1323), 89–92, 97
Hastings, family of, 24, 37–8
Hay, family of, 71, 81, 136
Henry III, King of England (d. 1272), 20–1, 26
Hestan Island, 128, *134*
Holyrood Abbey, 98, 100, 113
homage, for Scotland, 19, 22, 37–8, 41, 97–8, 139, *42*

Inverlochy Castle, 48, 68, *69*
Inverurie, battle of (1308), 68
Ireland, 16, 28, 51, 66–7, 82–5 [Bruce invasion], 92, 99, 149
Isabella, Countess of Buchan, 64, 66
Isabella, heiress of Fife, 112–4, 133
Isabella, Queen of England, 95–9, 105

Jean II, King of France (d. 1364), 141–2
Joan, Queen of Scots (d. 1362), 97–8, 107, 122, 133, 139, 146
John, Earl of Chester (d. 1237), 20, 23
Justiciars, Scottish, 17, 24, 62, 127, 133

Keith, Robert, the Marischal, and family of (d. 1346), 62, 71, 81, 92, 94, 109, 121, 136
Kildrummy Castle, 66, 112, 117, 119, *124*
Kinghorn, Fife, 22, 109, *27*
Kintyre, 40, 64, 66, 132

Lamberton, William, Bishop of St Andrews, Guardian of Scotland (d. 1328), 12, 51, 53–4, 56, 58, 60–2, 94, 106
Lancaster, earls/earldom of, 75, 85, 89
Lauder, Robert of the Bass, 92, 109
Lennox, earls/earldom of, 64, 81, 113
Lewes, battle of (1264), 21, 26, 44
Liddesdale, lordship of, 86, 131, 148
Lochmaben Castle, 54, 73, 138
Logie of Logie/Strathgartney, family of, 86, 133
Lothian(s), 16, 123, 128, 131–3, 136, 142
Loudon Hill, battle of, 1307, 67

MacCans, family of, 69, 73
MacDonald of Islay/Lord of the Isles, family of, 31, 41, 46, 48, 67, 69, 83–4, 94, 114, 132, 139, *84*
Macdougall, family of, 27, 30, 40–1, 48, 56, 66, 69, 73, 83–4, 99, 105, 115, 139
Macdowell, family of, 56, 67, 73, 83, 105, 128
MacDuffs of Fife, family of, 42, 48
MacRuaridh of Garmoran, family of, 67, 83–4, 94, 135, 139
Malcolm III, King of Scots (d. 1093), 16–7
Malcolm IV, King of Scots (d. 1165), 18
Man, isle of, 34, 83, 99

Mar, earldom of, 35–6, 41, 56, 64, 81, 92, 119
Mar, Donald Earl of, Guardian of Scotland (d. 1332), 97, 108–9
Margaret, Maid of Norway (d. 1290), 22, 28, 30, 32–6, 82, *33*
Margaret, Saint, Queen of Scots (d. 1093), 16, 20, 135
Margaret, Queen of Scots (d. 1275), 21–2
Maxwell of Caerlaverock, family of, 86, 109, 128, *116*
Melrose, abbey of, 32, 86, 92, 132, *93, 96*
Menteith, earls/earldom of, 64, 81, 92, 133, 138
Menteith, family of Arran and Knapdale, 62, 74, 81
Menteith, Murdoch of, 85, 109
Menzies, family of, 81, 121
Methven, battle of (1306), 66
Moray, earldom of, 17, 36, 71, 119, 121, 146
Mowbray, family of, 26, 56, 62, 68, 73, 86, 105, 108, 112, 115, 117
Murray, Andrew Bishop of Brechin, 94, 109
Murray, Andrew (d. 1297), 48, 50–1, 112
Murray, Andrew of Bothwell, Avoch and Garioch, Guardian of Scotland (d. 1338), 92, 112, 115, 117–8, 119–24, 126, *120*
Murray of Tullibradine, family of, 109, 128
Murray, Maurice, of Drumsargard, Earl of Strathearn (d. 1346), 128, 132, 136

national identity, Scottish, 13–4, 88, 111–2, 139, 146–9
Neville's Cross, battle of (1346), 129, 135–8, *130*
Norham, Castle/Process of, 1291, 36–7, 89, 96–7, 142, 148, *37*
Northmberland/Northumbria, 15–28, 36, 75, 114
Norway/the Norse, 21–1, 32–4, 43–4, 66

Ordinance for Government of Scotland (1305), 61–2
Otterburn, battle of (1388), 149

Papacy/Popes, 13, 19–20, 34, 51, 53, 55–6, 60, 72, 87–8, 94, 97, 99, 107, 122
Parliament, Scottish, 24 [1238?]; 22, 28, 30 [1284]; 29–30 [1286]; 36–7 [1291]; 40–1 [1292–6]; 53–4 [1299–1300]; 62 [1305]; 70–2 [1309]; 76 [1313]; 78 [1314]; 82 [1315]; 79, 85 [1318]; 85–6, 102 ['Black' Parliament, 1320]; 93 [1325]; 92–4 [1326]; 98–100 [1328]; 106–7 [1331]; 113 [1334]; 117 [1335]; 126 [1339]; 131 [council 1342]; 132–3 [1344]; 141–2 [1352]
peace terms, Anglo-Scottish, 91 [1323],

98–100 [1328], 137–46 [1346–71]

Percy, family of, 81, 98–9, 108, 138–9

Perth, 55, 73–4, 108–10, 112–4, 117, 121–3, 127

Philip IV, King of France, 43, 53, 55, 105

Philip VI, King of France, 114, 122–3, 127, 134

Poitiers, battle of (1356), 142–3

propaganda, Bruce (see also: Acts of Succession; Declarations), 36, 72, 86, 147–9

Quitclaim of Canterbury (1189), 20

Ramsay, Alexander of Dalhousie (d. 1342), 131–3

Ramsay, William, of Colluthie, 142

Randolph, John, Earl of Moray, Guardian of Scotland (d. 1346), 112, 114–7, 125, 131, 133–4, 136

Randolph, Thomas, Earl of Moray, Guardian of Scotland (d. 1332), 71, 74–8, 81–5, 92, 94, 97, 103, 104–7, 110

Randolph, Thomas, Earl of Moray (d. 1332), 109

Ross, Hugh Earl of (d. 1333), 94, 106, 113

Ross, William (II) Earl of (d. 1323), 66, 68, 70, 81

Ross, William (III) Earl of (d. 1371), 121, 127–9, 132–3, 135

Roxburgh, 50, 73–4, 97, 118, 122, 131, 138, 143, 149

St Andrew(s), 20, 39, 46, 70–2, 107, 109, 122–3, 31

Salisbury, treaty of (1289), 34

Scone, 18, 39, 41, 62, 64, 99, 106, 108–9, 126, 132, 141, 45

Seton, Sir Alexander (d. 1348), 76, 81, 92, 112

Seton, Sir Christopher (d. 1306), 62, 64, 66

sheriffs, Scottish, 17, 40, 47, 61–2, 71

Sinclair, William, Bishop of Dunkeld, 109

Skye, 40, 132

Soules, family of and conspiracy (1320), 17, 27, 30, 73, 85–6, 103, 105, 107, 109, 133, 149

Soules, John, Guardian of Scotland, 43, 56

Soules, William of Liddesdale, 78, 85–6, 131

Stewart, family of, 16, 31, 81, 139

Stewart, James, the Steward (d. 1309), 12, 31–2, 44, 50, 54, 56, 64, 66, 81, 92

Stewart, Robert, the Steward, King's Lieutenant (1335, 1338–41, 1347–57), King of Scots (1371–90), 85–6, 92, 106, 108, 112, 114–7, 125–29, 131–6, 138–9, 142–3, 146–9

Stewart, Thomas of Bonkil, Earl of Angus and family of, 81, 92, 107, 142

Stewart, Walter, the Steward (d. 1327), 81, 85, 106

Stirling/Stirling Castle/Bridge, battle of, 1297, 31, 55, 55, 60–1, 73–4, 76–8, 112–3, 122–3, 128

Strathbogie, family/lordship of, 92, 99, 119, 139

Strathbogie, David Earl of Atholl (d. 1306), 35–6, 41, 54, 64, 66

Strathbogie, David Earl of Atholl (d. 1326), 71, 73–4, 76

Strathbogie, David Earl of Atholl (d. 1335), 105–6, 108, 114–7, 119–21, 126

Strathearn, earls/earldom of, 24, 30, 41, 46, 81, 109, 126–7, 132, 138, 146

Strathearn, Malise (VII), Earl of, 48, 66, 73–4

Strathearn, Malise (VIII), Earl of, 74, 85, 107–9, 113, 126–7, 132

succession, Scottish, 18, 79–82, 85, 133–4, 139–42, 146–7, 149

Sutherland, John (d. 1361), 133–4

Sutherland, William Earl of, 121, 133–4, 136

Sweetheart Abbey, 100, 96

Tower of London, 11, 19, 46, 64, 136–7, 141

Troup, Hamelin de, 86, 109

truce, Anglo-Scottish, 86–8 [1319–21], 92–3 [1323–7]

Turnberry Band/Castle, 1286, 31, 66, 100

Ulster, earls/earldom of, 31, 55, 60, 66, 83–4, 92, 97, 99–100, 57

Umphraville, family of, 24, 30, 73, 105, 108, 113

Umphraville, Ingelram de, Guardian of Scotland, 43, 54, 56, 78, 85–6, 149

Urquhart Castle, 47–8, 68, 117

Wales, 16, 44, 51, 72, 82, 119

Wallace, William, Guardian of Scotland (d. 1305), 11–2, 14, 48, 50–53, 60–2, 66, 92, 112, 148, 49

Westminster, 21, 42, 61–2, 74, 76, 99, 128, 45

Wigtown, 13, 24, 31, 82, 100

William I, the Lion, King of Scotland (d. 1214), 19–20, 23, 55

Wishart, Robert, Bishop of Glasgow, Guardian of Scotland (d. 1316), 30, 32, 37, 50–1, 61, 64, 66

Yolande of Dreux, Queen of Scotland, 22, 31

York/Yorkshire, 20–1, 23, 42, 75, 89, 97, 107, 112, 135, 144

THE BATTLE FOR ABERDEEN 1644
CHRIS BROWN
The first-ever history of the battle for Aberdeen
fought during the British Civil Wars.
128pp 72 illus. Paperback £12.99/$18.99
ISBN 0 7524 2340 1

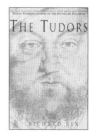

THE TUDORS
RICHARD REX
'The best introduction to England's
most important dynasty' *David Starkey*
272pp 120 illus. (30 col.) Paperback £16.99/$24.99
ISBN 0 7524 1971 4

BOSWORTH 1485: PSYCHOLOGY OF A BATTLE
MICHAEL K. JONES
'Transforms our understanding of what actually
happened on that fateful day' *Professor A.J. Pollard*
272pp 100 illus. (30 col.) Hardback £25/$29.99
ISBN 0 7524 2334 7

THE BATTLE OF HASTINGS 1066
M.K. LAWSON
A major re-interpretation
of the most decisive battle in English history.
272pp 120 illus. (25 col.) Paperback £16.99/$24.99
ISBN 0 7524 1998 6

THE BATTLE OF BANNOCKBURN 1314
ARYEH NUSBACHER
'The most accessible and authoritative book on the
battle' *Dr Fiona Watson, presenter of BBC TV's In Search
of Scotland*
176pp 73 illus. (16 col.) Paperback £12.99/$18.99
ISBN 0 7524 2326 6

FLODDEN 1513
NIALL BARR
'Reads as thrillingly as a novel' *The Scots Magazine*
176pp 74 illus. (23 col.) Paperback £16.99/$24.99
ISBN 0 7524 1792 4

UK ORDERING

Simply write, stating the quantity of books required and enclosing a cheque
for the correct amount, to: Sales Department, Tempus Publishing Ltd,
The Mill, Brimscombe Port, Stroud, Glos. GL5 2QG, UK.
Alternatively, call the sales department on 01453 883300 to pay by Switch, Visa or Mastercard.

US ORDERING

Please call Tempus Publishing toll free on 1-888-313-2665
or write to: Tempus Publishing Inc., 2 Cumberland Street, Charleston, SC 29401, USA